THE NEGRONI

the Negroni

DRINKING TO LA DOLCE VITA, WITH RECIPES & LORE

GARY "GAZ" REGAN

PHOTOGRAPHY BY KELLY PULEIO

TEN SPEED PRESS

BERKELEY

THIS BOOK IS DEDICATED TO AMY GALLAGHER,
MY ONE TRUE LOVE. LET'S SPIN THIS OUT FOR
ANOTHER COUPLE OF THOUSAND YEARS, BABE.

"CAN'T YOU SEE IT'S ALL PERFECT?"
-NEEB KARORI BABA (MARARAJ-JI)

CONTENTS

———

RECEIPE LIST

—

FOREWORD: PERFECTION KNOWS ITS PLACE

BY ROBERT SIMONSON

Ask bartenders what their favorite cocktail is, and 90 percent of the time they'll say one of two things: the old-fashioned or the Negroni.

For all the pyrotechnics and eleven-ingredient drinks of the twenty-first-century bar world, mixologists respect simplicity more than anything. And the old-fashioned and Negroni are as elemental as a drink can come. I am an old-fashioned man. But I am in sympathy with those who think the Negroni may be the perfect cocktail. Yes, the old-fashioned adheres, to the letter, to the classic definition of the cocktail: spirit, sugar, water, and bitters. But it doesn't possess that magical quality, owned by the Negroni (and few other drinks), of having located its sweet spot of balance and deliciousness in the equal proportion of its ingredients. One-third gin, one-third sweet vermouth, and one-third Campari: that's it—that's the Negroni in all its improbable poetry.

Within that three-decker arrangement, the Negroni manages to bring every taste bud into play. The gin provides its varied botanical bite. The vermouth lends a bit of sweet, a bit of spicy. Most critically, Campari brings on the bitter so beloved by a barkeep's sophisticated palate. Whatever sensation you're looking for in your cocktail, it's in there, and that dichotomy of variety within purity is what bewitches so many. Moreover, the Negroni gives each of these challenging ingredients a chance to shine. No member of the trio dominates; all have their say. The Negroni is a democracy.

As with the old-fashioned, the Manhattan, and other classics built on a sturdy foundation, the Negroni invites experimentation. Bartenders switch up the gin and vermouth brands and even sub out the spirit completely. (Thankfully, the Campari is rarely up for debate.) These fits of fancy often lead to interesting drinks (but, I'd argue, rarely better ones).

Although it's a relatively old drink, the Negroni's rise to prominence is recent. Perhaps the fact that it was invented on the eve of Prohibition explains why it didn't get much traction in the States until after World War II, when the drink began to appear in newspapers and restaurants on both coasts. But the Negroni's true heyday is now. A few years into the twenty-first century, the cocktail was everywhere. A turning point of sorts came when the restaurant Lincoln opened at the Lincoln Center and devoted an entire bar to the Negroni and its variations. (Curiously, the Negroni seems to be even more popular among chefs than it is with bartenders.) At this rate of ascendancy, the Negroni will graduate in a few years' time from its status as a secondary classic to the halcyon plane occupied by the martini, Manhattan, old-fashioned, and select other top-drawer cocktails. Perfection knows its place.

ACKNOWLEDGMENTS

I've known quite a few adequate editors in my time as a writer, and quite a few who do a good job, too. I've encountered only a few masters of the craft, though. Roy Finamore, editor of my baby, *The Joy of Mixology*, is one of them, and David Stevens (now retired) of *Playboy* magazine, is another. Jon Bonné, my editor at the *San Francisco Chronicle* for over a decade, consistently made my work far better than I ever could have managed on my own, and Martha Schueneman, my friend as well as my editor for many projects, also falls into this category. Nobody does it better, Ms. M.

Emily Timberlake, editor of this book and the woman who sought me out in order to get this particular show on the road, now joins Roy, David, and Martha at the very top of the editorial pyramid. You are uncannily fabulous and intuitive, Emily. I thank Great Spirit for putting us together.

Thanks also to the ever-thoughtful Robert Simonson (I treasure my silver "gaz" matchbox cover!) for such a fine foreword, and for being a true and loyal friend in the industry.

A huge thanks is due to photographer Kelly Puleio, who added so much depth and mood to these pages that I think I could live in this book very happily indeed, and to our designer, Margaux Keres, who also brought so much to this party that it's hard to imagine what the book would have looked like without her. Thanks, guys. You both rock.

And finally I'd like to thank, from the bottom of my Negroni-laden heart, each and every bartender who shared their recipes, and their thoughts on the Negroni, for this book. When we meet at that great stretch of mahogany in the sky, the first Negroni's on me.

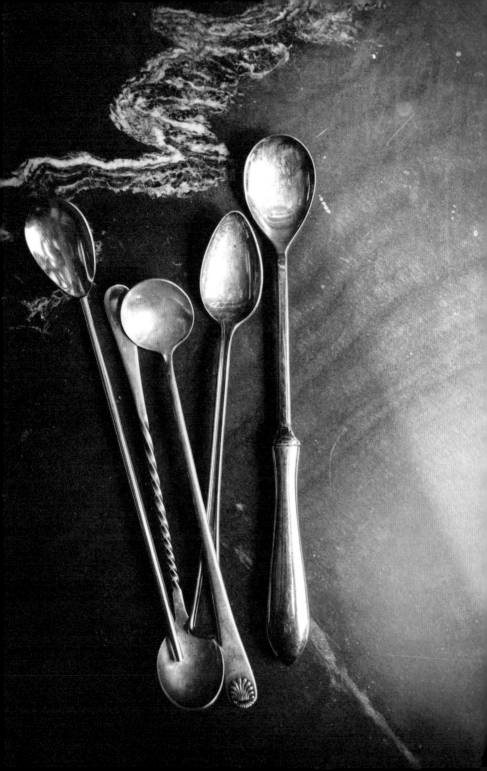

INTRODUCTION

> The crowning glory of Campari-based mixed drinks must be
> the Negroni. Made with equal parts gin, sweet vermouth,
> and Campari, the Negroni is traditionally served on the rocks
> with a slice of orange. So, at what point in a meal do I order
> my Negroni? Whenever I darned well feel like it. That's
> when. Sometimes it serves as my digestivo, sometimes it's
> my apéritif, and sometimes I order a Negroni when I have no
> plans to dine at all. It's a robust cocktail that's not as strong
> as, say, a martini, but it lets you know that you've had
> something substantial to drink. —Gary Regan

It may seem odd to start this book with an epigraph written by . . . me. The
quotation above is from a piece I wrote for *Los Angeles* magazine in September 2001. Yes, you read that right, 2001—well before the craft cocktail
craze, let alone the Negroni craze, that is currently sweeping the country
was in full swing. The title of my article was "Italian Sophistication: Bitter
Is Better," and I feel even more strongly about that assertion now than I did
nearly fifteen years ago.

I honestly don't remember my first Negroni, but I know that the Milanese
theory that one must drink Campari three times before starting to like it
certainly never applied to me. Campari was a love-at-first-sip sort of thing
for me. I've a passion for all things bitter—save for the odd ex-girlfriend.

The incredible aspect of the Negroni that not everyone understands—or
agrees with—is that it works every time, no matter what brand of gin or
sweet vermouth you use. And you can slap my wrist and call me Deborah
if it doesn't also work no matter what ratios you use.

Seriously, try it. Go up on the gin, the Campari, or the vermouth. These
three ingredients are soul mates, and they support each other no matter
how you try to fool them.

Personally, I go for a long-on-the-gin Negroni, and when I build them at home, which is very frequently, especially during the warmer months, I tend toward around four parts gin to one part each of sweet vermouth and Campari. I came up with this formula in 1999 for the very first issue of my *Ardent Spirits* email newsletter, which was published in February, just in time for Valentine's Day. Originally I called the drink the Valentino, but I soon gave that up. It's just a damned strong Negroni—the way I like 'em.

There are people who will argue that unless the drink is made with equal parts of the trinity that tumbles into the glass and unifies as a Negroni, it cannot be called a Negroni. I'll fight to the death for their right to say that, but they're wrong.

First, I need to point out that there is no regulatory board governing the names of drinks. And next, I should say that I believe we'd do ourselves a service by looking toward the world of food for guidance in this matter. After all, both chefs and bartenders are in the business of following or creating recipes, right?

If a chef makes a béarnaise sauce, do you think he or she first finds out how Jules Colette, the chef who created the sauce Paris in the 1800s, made his béarnaise? No, of course not. And neither do chefs go running to the library to find out the exact recipe for lobster thermidor as it was prepared at Marie's, the restaurant where the dish originated—again in Paris—to honor Victorien Sardou's play *Thermidor*.

I think it's important, whenever possible, to find out how specific cocktails were originally made. And in the case of the Negroni, we're lucky to have the 1:1:1 formula as a template. But each and every bartender out there, I think, enjoys putting his or her own twist on all of the classics, so let's not get bogged down in minutiae. Don't you love going to Tommy's for a margarita because they make their very own version of the drink there? And it's still a margarita, right?

And for those folk who still insist that the original formula is the only way to go, I applaud your stubbornness—and hope you've managed to locate the same brands of gin and vermouth as Count Negroni used back in 1919 . . .

For this book, I've traveled far and wide to ferret out the absolute best Negroni recipes—variations, riffs, abominations, whatever you want to call them—in the world. Some are pretty darned close to the gin-vermouth-Campari version we're all familiar with. Others swap in unusual and unexpected modifiers, base spirits, and amari. Some look and feel like a classic Negroni but reveal themselves to be strikingly different upon first sip. Others aren't even red. ("A *white* Negroni?" you say, aghast.)

What these drinks have in common is their complete and utter delicious-ness. And they all owe their existence to the same forefather; they were all built on the same foundation. That foundation is the Negroni, born in Italy (we think), under circumstances that are still fiercely debated to this day, and which I will try to outline for you in the pages that follow.

PART ONE

THE LORE

the one & only
Count Negroni

There was a time, not too very long ago, when I thought Count Negroni was a myth, possibly created by some marketers working for the good folk at Campari. I was wrong.

In relatively recent years, David Wondrich, author of *Imbibe!*—possibly the best cocktail book ever written—discovered what I and most others believe to be the true story of the birth of the Negroni in an Italian book, *Sulle tracce del conte: La vera storia del cocktail "Negroni"* (*On the Count's Trail: The Real Story of the Negroni Cocktail*), written by Luca Picchi, head bartender at Caffè Rivoire in Florence, Italy. The book was first published in 2000, and Luca Picchi tirelessly researched family archives, newspaper accounts, and countless old documents in order to write it. He's working on a new edition as I write this book, and there are rumors that an English-language edition is also in the works.

It turns out that there actually was an Italian count by the name of Camillo Negroni, and he was the guy who took the soda out of the Americano (Campari, sweet vermouth, and club soda) and added gin to the mixture to give it more of a kick.

NEGRONI FOREBEARS: THE AMERICANO, TORINO-MILANO, AND MILANO-TORINO

But let me back up for a moment here, because really no story about the Negroni makes sense without first introducing the Americano, its most immediate precursor. Just as we'd have no martini if it weren't for the Martinez, the Negroni might never have been born if the Americano hadn't been in place. Made by simply mixing Campari, sweet vermouth, and club soda, the Americano (page 33) was all the rage in Italy during the teen years of the twentieth century, so this is one of the drinks that Count Negroni would have encountered when he returned from his tour of the wild and wooly West (more about that later). American-style drinks were sweeping Europe at the time, and it was de rigueur to be seen with your fist firmly around a glass of something American.

That said, it's also important to note that Italians already had a firm grasp on *aperitivi* and *digestivi*—drinks known to the French as aperitifs and digestifs, intended to be sipped before or after a meal. These categories of drinks included brandies and eaux-de-vie, of course, but in Italy there was a leaning toward amari: bitter drinks, flavored with all manner of herbs, spices, and fruits, that had been popular there since the first commercial vermouth was released by Antonio Benedetto Carpano of Turin in 1786.

Although vermouth isn't really considered to be an amaro, its creation almost certainly led to the invention of quaffs such as Cynar, Fernet-Branca, and, of course, the star of this book, Campari. Once producers saw a market for bitter drinks such as these, they jumped on the amari bandwagon, so to speak, and made their presence known.

One very logical story about the creation of the Americano comes from Dom Costa, a celebrated Italian bartender and good friend of mine, who says that the Americano was based on a drink known in Italy as the Milano-Torino (page 32), a simple mixture of Campari (from Milan) and Martini & Rossi sweet vermouth (from Turin). Add a little club soda, and you have an Americano.

Dom Costa also maintains that we should go just a little further back and take a look at the Torino-Milano (page 30), a drink that's well worth getting to know. It's made with equal parts of Campari and Amaro Cora, another fabulous Italian bitter that has a wonderful floral nose and hints of orange and cinnamon on the palate. So thanks to Dom Costa, we now know that the Negroni was born from the loins of the Americano, the Americano was based on the Milano-Torino, and the Milano-Torino, in turn, was a variation on the Torino-Milano.

ROPIN', RIDIN', GAMBLIN', AND DRINKIN' WITH COUNT NEGRONI

Flash-forward to Florence, Italy, circa 1919. The Americano, like the Milano-Torino and Torino-Milano before it, had long been in fashion at Italian cafés. A man walks into his favorite bar, Caffè Casoni, and orders a drink from a bartender there by the name of Fosco Scarselli. The man was Count Negroni, who, by the way, had traveled around the United States and made a living as a rodeo cowboy for a time. We can presume, then, that he was a tough man, so the proposition that he asked Scarselli to replace the soda in an Americano with gin makes a great deal of sense, right? Sounds like my kind of guy, Count Negroni.

But who is this Count Negroni, and what do we know of him?

Leave it to cocktail expert and archivist extraordinaire David Wondrich to dig up one of the only known historical accounts of the count, written in 1928 by a journalist named Bob Davis for the *Spokane Chronicle.*

In the account, we find Davis lost on the back roads of the Italian country-side, being driven by an Italian-speaking chauffeur with whom he cannot communicate. Frustrated, Davis leaves the car—and soon stumbles across a striking figure on horseback.

"There is nothing unusual about a man astride a cayuse, but when the rider wears a quirt [a short-handled riding whip with a braided leather lash] looped to his right wrist and the horse is champing a Spanish bit and is covered well up on the withers with a Mexican saddle, it is a signal—at least to me—that my native tongue is due and collectible," Davis writes.

"'You speak English,' I said boldly.

"'You're tootin' I do, hombre.'"

The man turned out to be none other than Count Camillo Negroni, who had traveled in the United States from the late 1880s until he returned to Italy in 1905. According to Negroni, in the States he "learned enough about stud, keno, and faro to get broke and stay that way. Punching horses suited me to death and I went adventuring over the ranges . . . I roughed it plenty; rode herd up through the Yellowstone country and wound up in the province of Alberta, Canada, horning in at the Oxley ranch."

When Negroni reveals his name, Davis is struck by a bolt of recognition: "Are you not the Count Camillo Negroni who, about 1898, with the then champion of the world turned a handful of chicken feed into $7,000-odd dollars at the Jamaica race track? I remember a dinner you and Fitz gave at Hahn's restaurant on Park Row in celebration of the great clean-up. Unless I am very much mistaken the whole wad was carefully removed from your estate in an uptown poker game."

What do we learn from this exchange? For one thing, that there most certainly existed a man named Count Negroni, who was a bit of a legend in the States for his cowboy persona, penchant for gambling, and love of great parties. While the article makes no mention of the count's eponymous drink, it's not hard to imagine that he would have returned to Italy from New York (by way of the Wild West) and demanded that his bartender swap in gin for the paltry club soda called for in an Americano.

Wondrich's research also reveals that Count Negroni was born Camillo Luigi Manfredo Maria Negroni in Florence on May 25, 1868, to Count Enrico Negroni and Ada Savage Landor. After his legendary stint in the States, he returned to Florence, where he would for the most part stay

until his death on September 25, 1934. Some researchers still question whether or not he was a true "count," although Wondrich points out that his father, Enrico Negroni, was the son of Count Luigi Negroni and Countess Sofia Rusca. But either way, I believe we can all thank Signor Negroni for his contribution to our alcoholic heritage—and David Wondrich for his generosity in making the aforementioned newspaper account available to me for this book.

WHAT? ANOTHER COUNT NEGRONI?

Negroni, it turns out, was not an entirely uncommon surname back in those days. In fact, there's another Count Negroni—and one of his descendants insists that *he* was the man who first created the cocktail.

The second Count Negroni was, in fact, General Pascal Olivier Count de Negroni, who, according to his relative Noel Negroni, was born in the castle of San Colombano on April 4, 1829, and died in Alençon, Orne, on October 22, 1913. Noel writes, "Pascal joined the French Army at eighteen years of age and retired as a brigadier general after a long, illustrious career spanning forty-four years. He is best remembered in the French Army annals for leading the legendary charge of cuirassiers in the Battle of Reichshoffen during the Franco Prussian War of 1870. As a reward for his valiant actions and exemplary conduct, he was personally decorated on August 20, 1870, by the French emperor, Louis-Napoléon, with the Officer's Cross of the Imperial Legion of Honor. On September 3, 1870, he was captured by the Prussians during the Battle of Sedan and spent time as a prisoner of war until his liberation on March 28, 1871. On December 27, 1884, he was promoted to brigadier general, and on May 4, 1889, he was named commander of the Legion of Honor. In 1891 he retired to Château de Rochefeuille, near Mayenne, France. Pascal Olivier was the reputed inventor of the famous 'Negroni Cocktail' (equal parts of Campari, gin, and sweet vermouth, served in a short glass over ice and garnished with an orange slice)."

OH, CHE BEL PAESAGGIO!

In 1984, Federico Fellini, the Italian movie director known for his beautiful flights of fantasy in movies such as $8\frac{1}{2}$ and *Satyricon*, produced a commercial for Campari. Search YouTube and you shall find it. The piece, called *Oh, che bel paesaggio!* (Oh, what a beautiful landscape!), is set on a train and features a smiling, bearded middle-aged man, played by Victor Poletti, and a young woman who seems to be very annoyed, played by Silvia Dionisio. Using what looks like a remote control for a television, the woman keeps changing the landscape outside the train window. She eventually throws the remote to the older guy, who uses it to show her some Italian landmarks, Campari being one of them. Pretty cool, huh?

There is no doubt that this second Negroni led a very storied and illustrious life. But the only question that interests us here is whether he invented the signature drink.

Careful readers will recall that I said Count Negroni invented the cocktail circa 1919—and that Noel Negroni admits that his ancestor died in 1913. That birth date of the Negroni cocktail didn't come from thin air; in a forum post at the website of the Chanticleer Society, David Wondrich offered this careful study of the drink's origins:

> Besides the account of Fosco Scarselli, barman at the Caffè Casoni, Cammillo's regular watering-hole, that the drink was created when, one day between 1919 and 1920, Count Camillo (at some point he dropped the second m in his name) came into the bar and asked him to *irrobustire* (fortify) his customary Americano with gin, there's also a photograph of an October 13, 1920, letter in English addressed to "My Dear Negroni" by Frances Harper of Chelsea, London. In it appear the following lines:
>
> "You say you can drink, smoke, & I am sure laugh, just as much as ever [evidently Negroni had been ill]. I feel you are not much to be pitied! You must not take more than 20 Negronis in one day!"
>
> According to Scarselli, the count made frequent pit-stops at the bar and was often good for as many as 40 Negronis a day, so 20 represents an austerity program.
>
> Short of sworn testimony, photographs, and notarized depositions, this is about as good as evidence of the origins of a classic cocktail can get.

———

On Facebook, the famous Italian bartender Dom Costa made his own case for Camillo Negroni's authorship of the drink:

> The cocktail Negroni is without any shadow of doubt created in Florence between 1919 and 1920 at the Caffè Casoni located in Via Tornabuoni. This is it! There are no other stories, doubts, replies, or documents that may say otherwise: I have in my possession birth and death certificates, family tree, eight hundred photos, written statements of many Florentine bartenders of the past, plus an audio-taped statement by Franco Scarselli (son of Fosco), who really met Count Camillo Negroni. I also have hundreds of newspaper articles, both Italian and American, signed letters by the count himself, and artifacts and evidence from direct descendants of the count. It seems strange that a character who came out of nowhere and died in 1913 could have invented a cocktail in Corsica before it was even served in Florence's cafés, while in Corsica nobody even knows how to make a Negroni.

Fighting words, to be sure. For my part, I have to side with Wondrich and Costa. But wouldn't it be amazing if, one day, Noel Negroni's family turned up solid information to substantiate his claim? It seems too funny to think about, but stranger things have happened.

At this moment, though, I'm absolutely convinced that Camillo Negroni, the bronco buster, was the man who first put the Negroni together.

Campari, Negroni's Muse

It's possible to make a Negroni using one of thousands of different gins out there, and the choice of sweet vermouths is pretty vast these days, too. Each gin, and each vermouth, will bring its own nuances to the party, and some of these bottlings—think G'Vine Floraison gin or Carpano Antica Formula vermouth—will shape the drink into something completely different from a Negroni made with a traditional London dry gin (Beefeater, Broker's, or Tanqueray, for instance) or a less forthright but very flavorful vermouth (such as Martini & Rossi or Noilly Prat).

Mix and match your gins and vermouths, then, but if you want a true Negroni, the Campari stays. You might be able to make a variation on the drink using one of the many amari on the market, but without Campari, it just ain't a Negroni. Campari is a given in the Negroni. It's the defining ingredient.

Although the Campari company is pretty secretive about how they make their fine product, they did share some tidbits of information with me, which I'll now share with you:

> A unique and unmistakable recipe has characterized Campari, the aperitif par excellence, for over 150 years. The inimitable Campari recipe, used as the basis of many cocktails served worldwide, has been kept the same since its inception and remained a closely guarded secret, passed down over the years. Bitter all'Uso d'Holanda, as Campari was initially called, was the result of Gaspare Campari's experiments in concocting new beverages. It is still produced today with the same ingredients and following the confidential recipe which remains a secret known only to the very few people in charge of the production process. Campari is the result of the infusion of herbs, aromatic plants, and fruit in alcohol and water; these last two being the recipe's only known ingredients. Many have guessed simply at the number of ingredients: some say there are 20 or 60, but others list the ingredients at 80. Nobody knows the real answer apart from those who have passed down Gaspare's recipe for over 150 years.

So just who was Gaspare Campari, and how did he come to create his eponymous potion? Thereby hangs a tale.

In 1828, in the village of Castelnuovo, about twenty-two miles northwest of Milan, Gaspare Campari was born to a family of farmers. By the time he was fourteen years old, he was working at the Bass Bar in Turin as an apprentice *maître licoriste*, the equivalent of today's master mixologists. It wasn't too very long before Gaspare opened his own bar, making liqueurs and bitters in the basement. One of his signature liqueurs was known at the time as Bitter all'Uso d'Holanda, and this was to become his crowning glory, eventually becoming known as Campari—a drink that Gaspare was

CAMPARI'S UNIQUE BITTER
STOMATOLOGICAL CORDIAL

"Campari was the first to produce this Bitter all'uso d'Hollanda which was quickly appreciated by the public and has been imitated by nearly all other liqueur manufacturers. No one, however, has managed to recreate Campari's unique bitter stomatological [relating to the medical study of the mouth and its diseases] cordial whose immense turnover is proof of how the connoisseurs have appreciated its superior quality." From Gaspare Campari's application to display his goods at the trade fair Esposizione Industriale Italiana in 1880. *Thirty Years and a Century of the Campari Company*, Davide Campari, 1990.

BITTER RED

I love Campari, but their secrecy policies sometimes drive me crazy. Like many others before me, I wanted to know more about Campari's signature red color—why and how they make it so. When I asked, though, this was all I got: "Campari is a product with more than 150 years of history. Its signature ruby red color is an essential element. Prior to 2006, Campari used carmine as a coloring. Due to unpredictable fluctuations in both supply and quality, the company chose to no longer use carmine as it embarked on becoming a global brand. Campari's unique flavors and colorings remain proprietary information." What can we take away from this? Previously, Campari owed its hue to carmine, a red food coloring that comes from a type of beetle. Today, due to Campari's wild popularity and carmine supply issues, it's fair to assume they use artificial colorings. Vegans, rejoice!

so proud of, he decided it was good enough to bear his name. When he died in 1882, the *Corriere della Serra*, a Milanese newspaper that's still published today, declared him to have been "A Self-Made Man" on their front page. Such compliments were hard to come by.

Gaspare's sons, Davide and Guido Campari, then took over the company. Davide had worked for his father at Café Campari, the family's place in Milan, for over thirty years at that point, and it was he who possessed the marketing genius that would put Campari on the map worldwide. He commissioned famous artists to design posters for the company and only allowed cafés that promised to display Campari signs to sell his products.

In the early 1900s, Davide met Lina Cavalieri, a famous opera singer of the time. After falling in love with her and deciding to follow her around the world, he decided to incorporate a little business into his pleasure. He started to export Campari to each country he visited.

Today, over three million cases of Campari are sold worldwide each year, and it's available in almost two hundred countries. Thankfully, then, Negronis are available almost everywhere we travel these days. Methinks that Gaspare would have approved.

HOLY BOOZY TRINITY

"[The Negroni is] a punch-packing, bitter and sweet holy boozy trinity that, despite its complex flavors, may be the world's most foolproof cocktail."

—KEVIN SINTUMUANG, the *Wall Street Journal*, May 28, 2011

WHAT'S THAT *YOU'RE* DRINKING?

"If I were James Bond (an Italian Bond, of course), a Negroni would be my drink. It's a masculine drink, not sweet but with huge flavors. It commands the question, 'What's that *you're* drinking?' One reason I love this drink so much is that the bitter tinge gets your palate ready for a meal."

—*MICHAEL CHIARELLO'S BOTTEGA* by Michael Chiarello, with Ann Krueger Spivack and Claudia Sansone

PART TWO

THE RECIPES

the Classic Negronis

From every classic cocktail new cocktails arise. Some stay the course and stick around for decades; others drop to the wayside as wannabes that just couldn't cut it. Similarly, it's often possible to find drinks that predate classic formulas and offer clear insight into a drink's heritage. So where did the Negroni come from? How did it get here? In this selection of recipes, we'll look at both sides of that coin to gain perspective on our beloved Negroni.

We'll get to know its aunts, cousins, daughters, and stepbrothers. As you'll see, the Negroni family is a pretty diverse group.

CLASSIC 1:1:1 NEGRONI

I prefer juniper-heavy gins in my Negronis, hence Beefeater, G'Vine Nouaison, and Tanqueray lead the charge into my glass—and I tend to pour heavy when adding the gin, too. Vermouth-wise, I'm still a sucker for Noilly Prat sweet vermouth, finding it to be lush, round, and fruity, with none of the unwanted spice notes that are appearing in some of today's newer bottlings. Yes, Carpano Antica Formula, I'm talking about you!

Feel free to play with the ratios in this formula and make the drink your own. Remember, one of the cardinal rules when it comes to cocktail recipes: Nothing Is Written in Stone.

1 OUNCE GIN

1 OUNCE SWEET VERMOUTH

1 OUNCE CAMPARI

GARNISH: 1 ORANGE TWIST

Stir all the ingredients with ice in a double old-fashioned glass. Garnish with the orange twist.

TORINO-MILANO

Look here for the fabulous floral notes that Amaro Cora brings to this party in a glass. You'll likely find hints of orange zest and cinnamon, too.

1½ OUNCES AMARO CORA

1½ OUNCES CAMPARI

GARNISH: 1 ORANGE TWIST

Stir the amaro and Campari with ice in an old-fashioned glass. Garnish with the orange twist.

MILANO-TORINO

Martini Rosso is a great sweet vermouth, with a style that's lighter than the heavy berry notes found in, say, Noilly Prat. As such, it's a perfect sister for Campari, since each allows the other to tango in her own style, never bumping into each other and always keeping the same beat.

1½ OUNCES MARTINI ROSSO VERMOUTH

1½ OUNCES CAMPARI

GARNISH: 1 ORANGE TWIST

Stir the vermouth and Campari with ice in an old-fashioned glass. Garnish with the orange twist.

AMERICANO

Sorry to say that the Americano walks a different street than I, but if you're seeking a refreshing quaff, it might very well work for you. Whatever you do, though, don't even get your nose close to an Americano if there's no orange twist in there.

1½ OUNCES CAMPARI

1½ OUNCES SWEET VERMOUTH

2 OUNCES CLUB SODA

GARNISH: 1 ORANGE TWIST

Pour the ingredients, in the order above, into an ice-filled highball glass. Garnish with the orange twist.

THEY BALANCE EACH OTHER

One of the earliest reports of the Negroni came from Orson Welles in correspondence with the *Coshocton Tribune* while working in Rome on *Cagliostro* in 1947, where he described a new drink called the Negroni. He declared that the bitters (Campari) are excellent for the liver while the gin is bad for you. "They balance each other," he said.

NEGRONI SBAGLIATO

The house specialty at the legendary Bar Basso in Milan is the Negroni Sbagliato, which translates as "wrong" or "mistaken" Negroni—a fitting name for a cocktail born from a happy mistake. When making a Negroni in the late 1980s, a bartender grabbed a bottle of spumante instead of gin. The drink was an instant hit, and it soon became the bar's signature cocktail.

1 OUNCE SWEET VERMOUTH

1 OUNCE CAMPARI

1 OUNCE PROSECCO OR OTHER SPARKLING WINE

GARNISH: 1 ORANGE SLICE

Stir the vermouth and Campari with ice in an old-fashioned glass. Pour in the Prosecco and stir again. Garnish with the orange slice.

MY OLD PAL

According to Scotsman Adam Elmegirab, creator of Dr. Adam Elmegirab's Bitters, "The Old Pal, or 'My Old Pal,' first shows up in the 1922 edition of *Harry's ABC of Cocktails*. But oddly, in 1927, Arthur Moss credits the drink to one 'Sparrow' Robertson, sporting editor of the *New York Tribune*, in the appendix of Harry McElhone's *Barflies and Cocktails*."

Not solely due to its cloudy origins, this is one of those cocktail recipes that drives so-called experts absolutely mad. Most people will tell you that the Old Pal is made with Campari, dry vermouth, and rye whiskey—sort of a rye Negroni. But Adam's research complicates things a bit.

He notes that a conflicting recipe appears in the 1927 book: "I remember way back in 1878, on the thirtieth of February to be exact, when the writer was discussing the subject with my old pal 'Sparrow' Robertson and he said to yours truly, 'Get away with that stuff, my old pal, here's the drink I invented when I fired the pistol the first time at the Powderhall foot races and you can't go wrong if you put a bet down on ⅓ Canadian Club, ⅓ Eyetalian Vermouth, and ⅓ Campari,' and then he told the writer that he would dedicate this cocktail to me, and call it, My Old Pal."

There's no denying that My Old Pal has a Negroni-style template, but if Sparrow Robertson really did invent this drink in 1878, then the My Old Pal predates the Negroni by over forty years. Interesting trivia, if nothing else.

Now, here's where the modern-day expert's feathers will get ruffled: the 1927 book calls for "Eyetalian Vermouth," meaning *sweet* vermouth. Whatever type of vermouth you use, this cocktail works best with a good straight rye; try using Michter's, Rittenhouse 100, or Sazerac.

1½ OUNCES STRAIGHT RYE WHISKEY

1 OUNCE CAMPARI

1 OUNCE DRY VERMOUTH (FOR THE 1922 VERSION) OR SWEET VERMOUTH (FOR THE 1927 VERSION)

Stir all the ingredients with ice in a mixing glass, then strain into a chilled champagne flute.

BOULEVARDIER

Harry McElhone is such a rabble-rouser. In his 1927 book *Barflies and Cocktails*, he proclaims, "Now is the time for all good barflies to come to the aid of the party, since Erskinne (sic) Gwynne crashed in with his Boulevardier cocktail: ⅓ Campari, ⅓ Italian vermouth, ⅓ Bourbon whiskey." His Boulevardier—*like his My Old Pal!*—calls for sweet vermouth. Cocktail purists will probably try to tell you that the Old Pal *has* to be made with dry vermouth and that the Boulevardier *has* to be made with sweet vermouth. I say pour me a drink and let's move on.

Actually, let's pause for a moment to reflect upon the Boulevardier. The name is a nod to a Parisian magazine along the lines of the *New Yorker*. The Erksine McElhone speaks of was the son of Edward Erskine and Helen Steele Gwynne, and his great-uncle was Cornelius Vanderbilt. Erskine was a wealthy man, as one might imagine.

Erskine's sister, Alice "Kiki" Gwynne, was a notorious drug addict, often referred to as "the girl with the silver syringe," and one of her three children was thought to have been fathered by Prince George, Duke of Kent, one of King George V of England's sons. The *Boulevardier* magazine began publication in 1927 (the same year in which *Barflies and Cocktails* hit the shelves), and while lofty writers such as Ernest Hemingway and Noel Coward were contributing to its pages, the proud publisher undoubtedly quaffed quality cocktails in the City of Lights.

1 OUNCE BOURBON	**1 OUNCE CAMPARI**
1 OUNCE SWEET VERMOUTH	**GARNISH: 1 ORANGE SLICE, LEMON TWIST, OR CHERRY**

Stir all the ingredients long and well with ice in a mixing glass, then strain into a cocktail glass. Garnish as desired.

the New Negronis

You'll find a broad range of Negroni variations in this chapter: some that are just slightly twisted, some that are quite similar to others but stamped with the signature of different bartenders, a few walking under the same name but with different formulas, and one or three recipes that, to be frank, are a bit of a stretch as Negroni variations. I included all of them so that this book might serve as one-stop shopping for anything and everything surrounding the fabulous drink we know fondly as the Negroni.

One of my aims in recent years has been to try to make recipes interesting by including the thoughts of a formula's creator whenever possible, by commenting on the drink myself, and by interspersing quotations and quips among the recipes. Hope you like it.

WHITE NEGRONI

ADAPTED FROM A RECIPE BY ERIC ALPERIN,
CO-OWNER OF THE VARNISH, LOS ANGELES

Eric didn't claim to have created this variation, and I'm told by Jim Meehan (owner of the New York City bar PDT) that it was English bartending legend Wayne Collins who first came up with the basic formula. Sorry, Wayne—I found this out at the very last minute.

Eric's tale of first serving this drink is worth telling, though: "When we opened the Varnish, we couldn't get Suze . . . so my lovely French mother was suitcase importing it for us. The best was when I got a shipment and the bottles were wrapped in my old socks and underwear which I'd left at home as a young man heading out on his own. Thanks, Mom . . ."

1½ OUNCES PLYMOUTH GIN	**¾ OUNCE SUZE**
¾ OUNCE DOLIN DRY VERMOUTH	**GARNISH: 1 GRAPEFRUIT TWIST**

Stir all the ingredients with ice in a double old-fashioned glass. Garnish with the grapefruit twist.

WHITE NEGRONI
WITH CAMPARI CAVIAR

BRIAN FELLEY AND MO HODGES, BENJAMIN-COOPER, SAN FRANCISCO

Here's another White Negroni variation, this one from bartenders at the sadly shuttered San Francisco bar Big. Making the Campari Caviar involves some black-belt bartending moves, but the result is a sight to behold.

2 OUNCES GIN	2 DASHES ORANGE BITTERS
½ OUNCE DOLIN DRY VERMOUTH	GARNISH: CAMPARI CAVIAR
½ OUNCE SALERS GENTIANE APERITIF	(RECIPE FOLLOWS) SECURED IN A GRAPEFRUIT TWIST

Stir all the ingredients with ice in a mixing glass, then strain into a chilled rocks glass. Form the grapefruit twist into a cone shape, secure with a cocktail pick, then fill with a spoonful of Campari Caviar. Position the cone on the side of the glass and serve.

———

CAMPARI CAVIAR

18 OUNCES WATER	1 OUNCE LUXARDO MARASCHINO LIQUEUR
2 OUNCES CAMPARI	
2 OUNCES COMBIER CRÈME DE PAMPLEMOUSSE ROSÉ LIQUEUR	1.5 GRAMS SODIUM ALGINATE
	5 GRAMS CALCIUM LACTATE

Combine 3 ounces of the water, the Campari, the Crème de Pamplemousse liqueur, the maraschino liqueur, and the sodium alginate. In a separate large bowl, combine the remaining 15 ounces of water with the calcium lactate to form a bath. Use a dropper to slowly drop the Campari mixture into the bath. Let the Campari droplets set for about 30 seconds (the longer they set, the firmer they will become). Remove the caviar from the bath with a strainer and rinse under cold water.

BITTER FRENCH

PHILIP WARD, MAYAHUEL, NEW YORK CITY

This is a sort of marriage between a French 75 (a classic drink that combines gin, citrus, and champagne) and a Negroni. Nice touch, Phil. It's almost like you know what you're doing . . .

1 OUNCE PLYMOUTH GIN

¼ OUNCE CAMPARI

½ OUNCE FRESH LEMON JUICE

½ OUNCE SIMPLE SYRUP (1:1 SUGAR:WATER)

CHAMPAGNE

GARNISH: 1 GRAPEFRUIT TWIST

Shake the gin, Campari, lemon juice, and simple syrup with ice, then strain into a chilled champagne flute. Top with champagne. Squeeze the grapefruit twist over the drink, then discard.

DISPATCHES FROM A CAMPARI RED BAR

The next four recipes all come from Shawn Soole of Little Jumbo Restaurant & Bar in Victoria, British Columbia. When the first edition of this book came out, Shawn was working at Clive's Classic Lounge in Victoria, Canada's first Campari Red Bar, a designation given to bars that Campari's head office feels are the best places to drink Campari. Shawn has since moved on to Little Jumbo, which opened in August 2013. In these recipes, he carries on the Negroni tradition in fine form.

DRUNK UNCLE

1½ ounces Islay
Scotch whisky, such
as Bowmore or
Laphroaig

¾ ounce Martini
Bianco

¾ ounce Cynar

Garnish: 1 grapefruit
twist

Stir all the ingredients with ice in a mixing glass, then strain into a chilled cocktail glass. Garnish with the grapefruit twist. (*Pictured on page 82.*)

MAXIMO DI NEGRONI

1 ounce
Beefeater 24 gin

1 ounce Punt e Mes

1 ounce Amaro
Nonino

Garnish: 1 orange
twist

Stir all the ingredients with ice in an old-fashioned glass. Garnish with the orange twist.

MINIMO DI NEGRONI

1 ounce Plymouth Gin Infused with Saffron (recipe follows)

1 ounce Cinzano Orancio vermouth

1 ounce Ramazotti Amaro

Garnish: 1 orange twist

Pour the ingredients into an ice-filled old-fashioned glass, stir briefly, and add the garnish.

――――――

PLYMOUTH GIN INFUSED WITH SAFFRON

1 (750 ml) bottle Plymouth gin

2 grams (about 4 teaspoons) whole saffron threads

Combine the gin and saffron in a jar with a tight-fitting lid. Seal the jar and shake gently. Let infuse for about 8 hours or overnight. Strain through a double layer of dampened cheesecloth.

LEMON BALM NEGRONI

1 ounce Tanqueray Gin Infused with Lemon Balm (recipe follows)

1 ounce Martini Bianco

1 ounce Cynar

Garnish: 1 lemon twist

Stir all the ingredients with ice in an old-fashioned glass. Garnish with the lemon twist.

――――――

TANQUERAY GIN INFUSED WITH LEMON BALM

1 (750 ml) bottle Tanqueray London dry gin

1 cup fresh lemon balm

Combine the gin and lemon balm in a jar with a tight-fitting lid. Seal the jar and shake gently. Let infuse for about 8 hours or overnight. Strain through a double layer of dampened cheesecloth.

NEGRONI FIZZ

GRACE ROTH, ADIRONDACK / KINFOLK 94, BROOKLYN

This cocktail riffs on the beloved formula of the ice cream float, but instead of root beer we get a boozy cocktail, and instead of cloying vanilla ice cream we get grown-up lemon sorbet. Grace says, "The bittersweet bite of the Campari is mellowed by the savory sweetness from the rosemary syrup, and topping it with a scoop of lemon sorbet not only keeps your cocktail cold (eliminating the need for ice), but also adds dimension to the flavor as it melts."

1 OUNCE GIN

1 OUNCE CAMPARI

1 OUNCE FRESH GRAPEFRUIT JUICE

1 TABLESPOON ROSEMARY SIMPLE SYRUP (RECIPE FOLLOWS)

CLUB SODA

1 SCOOP LEMON SORBET

GARNISH: 1 ROSEMARY SPRIG AND 1 GRAPEFRUIT TWIST

Shake the gin, Campari, grapefruit juice, and rosemary syrup with ice and strain into an old-fashioned glass. Top with club soda and the lemon sorbet, then garnish and serve.

———

ROSEMARY SIMPLE SYRUP

½ CUP WATER

½ CUP SUGAR

5 ROSEMARY SPRIGS

Combine the ingredients in a small saucepan over medium-high heat. Bring to a boil, turn the heat down to allow the mixture to simmer, and cook, stirring frequently, until the sugar dissolves, about 5 minutes. Remove from the heat and allow to cool completely, then strain through a double layer of cheesecloth.

BELFAST BASTARD

JACK MCGARRY, THE DEAD RABBIT, NEW YORK CITY

McGarry says, "This light, summery drink is a riff on the Lucien Gaudin, which I came up with a while back when I became aware of Combier's Crème de Pamplemousse Rose liqueur." Crème de Pamplemousse Rose, made with red grapefruit and neutral alcohol, has the refreshing flavor of very ripe grapefruit.

2 OUNCES TANQUERAY LONDON DRY GIN

½ OUNCE DOLIN DRY VERMOUTH

½ OUNCE CAMPARI

½ OUNCE COMBIER CRÈME DE PAMPLEMOUSSE ROSÉ LIQUEUR

2 DASHES REGANS' ORANGE BITTERS NO. 6

GARNISH: 1 GRAPEFRUIT TWIST

Stir all the ingredients with ice in a mixing glass, then strain into a chilled champagne coupe. Squeeze the grapefruit twist over the drink, then discard the twist and serve naked. (I'm not sure whether Jack is naked when he serves this, or if he is perhaps referring to the fact that the twist never makes it into the glass. I don't really want to find out . . .)

CORN GODDESS

ADAPTED FROM A RECIPE BY DAVID WONDRICH,
COCKTAIL HISTORIAN EXTRAORDINAIRE AND AUTHOR OF *IMBIBE!*
ALONG WITH OTHER MASTERFUL WORKS

Only Dave Wondrich could come up with a recipe as wacky as this one. And he made it work, too!

2 TABLESPOONS FRESH CORN KERNELS

2 CHERRY TOMATOES, HALVED

1 OUNCE GIN

1½ OUNCES CAMPARI

GARNISH: 1 FRESH SAGE LEAF

In a mixing glass, muddle the corn and tomatoes with the gin. Add ice and the Campari and shake well. Double strain into a chilled cocktail glass. Float the sage leaf on top of the drink.

AGENT PROVOCATEUR

FRANCESCO LAFRANCONI, SOUTHERN WINE & SPIRITS, LAS VEGAS

This recipe displays my friend Francesco's creative genius at its finest. He says you can use any base spirit here. The classic gin certainly works, as does rye, tequila, vodka, aquavit, Irish whiskey, scotch, or rum—you name it!

VARNELLI L'ANICE SECCO
SPECIALE LIQUEUR

1 OUNCE BASE SPIRIT (YOUR CHOICE)

1 OUNCE CAMPARI

½ OUNCE YELLOW CHARTREUSE

½ OUNCE LUXARDO
APRICOT LIQUEUR

GARNISH: 1 LEMON TWIST
AND 1 ORANGE TWIST

Rinse a chilled cocktail glass with the Varnelli l'Anice Secco Speciale liqueur, then discard. Stir the remaining ingredients with ice in a mixing glass, then strain into the cocktail glass. Squeeze both twists over the drink, then discard.

OAXACA NEGRONI

JOSH TRABULSI, BURRITT ROOM, SAN FRANCISCO

It's amazing how well the mezcal works in this drink. It's a very difficult spirit to integrate into cocktails, but here it's right at home in the glass.

1 OUNCE DEL MAGUEY VIDA MEZCAL

1 OUNCE COCCHI BAROLO CHINATO

1 OUNCE CAMPARI

GARNISH: 1 THIN ORANGE WHEEL

Stir all the ingredients with 1 large ice cube in a double old-fashioned glass. Garnish with the orange wheel.

MORE PICKY THAN MARTINI DRINKERS

"After a dozen years of bartending, I graduated to drinking Negronis in the late 1980s. It was probably my first 'adult' mixed drink. Over the years, I've learned how particular Negroni customers can be—often more picky than martini drinkers. In 1990 I started tending bar at Seattle's iconic Italian restaurant and bar, Il Bistro. There, I grew to prefer my Negronis made with Punt e Mes in place of sweet vermouth. I passed the recipe on to Nancy Leson, restaurant reviewer for the *Seattle Weekly*. Currently, Nancy writes for the *Seattle Times* online, and her husband still drinks his Negronis with Punt e Mes."

—MURRAY STENSON, Canon Whiskey and Bitters
Emporium, Seattle

NEGRONI WESTERN, PAGE 65

BITTER END

TED KILGORE, TASTE BAR AND LAST WORD COCKTAIL CONSULTING, ST. LOUIS

Ted has a cocktail style all his own, and he tends to go heavy on the octanes. But he ropes himself in here, just a little, and the resultant drink is, as we said in the seventies, "ice cool in space, baby!"

1½ OUNCES GIN

¾ OUNCE MARTINI & ROSSI BIANCO VERMOUTH

½ OUNCE CAMPARI

¼ OUNCE GREEN CHARTREUSE

¼ OUNCE AMARO NONINO

¾ OUNCE FRESH ORANGE JUICE

GARNISH: 1 FLAMED ORANGE TWIST

Shake all the ingredients with ice for 20 seconds—shake hard! Then strain into a chilled cocktail glass. Garnish with the flamed orange twist and savor the delicious bitterness!

BROOKLYN HEIGHTS

MAXWELL BRITTEN, PRINCIPAL BARKEEP, MAISON PREMIERE, BROOKLYN;
ORIGINAL RECIPE STOLEN FROM ROBERT SIMONSON'S BLOG,
MAKE IT SIMPLE BUT SIGNIFICANT

A few years ago I found myself looking for cocktails named after New York City neighborhoods, and I stumbled upon Robert Simonson's blog, mentioned above, where I found a whole collection of suitable recipes. Robert agreed to allow me to use these, as long as I fessed up to having stolen them from his blog. Sounded like a good deal to me, so I ran with it! Thanks again, Robert.

CAMPARI, IN A MISTER	¼ OUNCE LUXARDO AMARO ABANO
1½ OUNCES RITTENHOUSE 100 RYE WHISKEY	½ OUNCE LUXARDO MARASCHINO LIQUEUR
½ OUNCE NOILLY PRAT DRY VERMOUTH	2 DASHES REGANS' ORANGE BITTERS NO. 6

Mist a chilled cocktail glass with Campari. Stir the remaining ingredients with ice in a mixing glass, then strain into the cocktail glass.

A SPIRITUAL HOME: MAURO MAHJOUB'S NEGRONI CLUB, MUNICH, GERMANY

I've met Mauro Mahjoub quite a few times, and a passionate bartender he is indeed. Head honcho at Mauro's Negroni Club in Munich, he claims to have made 300,000 Negronis in his twenty-five-year bar career, and in 2012 he was appointed a brand ambassador for Campari.

Here are a few words of Negroni wisdom straight from the ambassador's mouth: "Obviously I have my favorite Negroni—1 ounce Tanqueray gin, 1⅓ ounces Campari, and 1 ounce Punt e Mes, with a twist of lemon and an orange slice. I've invented something like fifty Negroni variations for our menu, and we have fifteen variations that are changed every couple of years. At Tales of the Cocktail, the premier annual cocktail conference, I tried to make the largest Negroni in the world with nine other Italian friends."

Here's a sampling of Mauro's Negronis. I think you'll agree they are pretty darned special.

NEGRONI CLUB

1 ounce vanilla vodka

⅔ ounce dry vermouth

1 ounce Campari

1 ounce Chambord

2 ounces ginger beer

Garnish: 1 orange twist

Stir the vodka, vermouth, Campari, and Chambord with ice in a double old-fashioned glass. Add the ginger beer and orange twist and stir briefly.

NEGRONI FUTURISTA

1 ounce sloe gin

1 ounce fino sherry

1 ounce Campari

Garnish: 1 lemon twist

Stir all the ingredients with ice in a double old-fashioned glass. Garnish with the lemon twist.

NEGRONI WESTERN

1 ounce bourbon

⅔ ounce Lillet rouge

1 ounce Campari

⅔ ounce Frangelico

2 drops chocolate
bitters

Garnish: 1 orange
twist and 1 chocolate-
dipped spoon

Stir all the ingredients with ice
in a double old-fashioned glass.
Garnish with the orange twist
and chocolate-dipped spoon.
(Melville Candy Company
makes chocolate-dipped spoons
and they're available online, but
you can also simply serve a little
bittersweet chocolate next to
the drink.) (*Pictured on page 61.*)

NEGRONI DEL NONNO

⅔ ounce Del Nonno
grappa

⅔ ounce Punt e Mes

1 ounce Campari

⅓ ounce St-Germain

Garnish: 1
cucumber slice

Stir all the ingredients with ice
in a double old-fashioned glass.
Garnish with the cucumber slice.

EAST INDIA NEGRONI

JIM MEEHAN, PDT, NEW YORK CITY

According to Jim, "Lustau's East India Solera sherry is similar in style to the fortified wine that botanist Joseph Banks might have stocked when he sailed with Captain James Cook, the British explorer, in the late 1700s, and it's a great stand-in for sweet vermouth in this sugarcane-based variation on the classic gin drink."

2 OUNCES BANKS 5-ISLAND RUM

¾ OUNCE LUSTAU EAST INDIA SOLERA SHERRY

¾ OUNCE CAMPARI

GARNISH: 1 ORANGE TWIST

Stir all the ingredients with ice in a mixing glass, then strain into a rocks glass over 1 large ice cube. Garnish with the orange twist.

BOTTECCHIA

KEVIN BURKE, HEAD BARMAN, COLT & GRAY, DENVER

Burke says, "When we created the Bottecchia cocktail, we wanted it to be a Negroni variation, but in the spirit of *Spinal Tap* we wanted to turn it up to 11. Fernet-Branca replaced the gin, and Cynar was swapped in for the sweet vermouth. The salt tempers the bitterness of the amaro and adds a distinct savory element. We named the drink after Ottavio Bottecchia, a young professional cyclist who won the Tour de France in 1924 and wore the yellow jersey for the entire race (fifteen consecutive days). His life was cut short when he was found dead in 1927 of unknown causes. He was a known Socialist, and his politics put him in unpopular company."

1 OUNCE FERNET-BRANCA

1 OUNCE CYNAR

1 OUNCE CAMPARI

SMALL PINCH OF KOSHER SALT

GARNISH: 1 FAT GRAPEFRUIT TWIST

Stir all the ingredients in a mixing glass without ice until the salt is dissolved. Add ice and stir, then strain into a chilled coupe. Squeeze the grapefruit twist over the drink, then discard.

HOUSE OF PAYNE

PHIL WARD, MAYAHUEL, NEW YORK CITY

Phil says, "This drink is named for Desmond Payne, who arguably makes the best gin in world." Desmond Payne is the master distiller for Beefeater gin. He's painstakingly exacting—and a creative mastermind if ever there was one. Hanging with Desmond can be a very educational experience. He's lots of fun, too!

1 FRESH RASPBERRY

1 OUNCE CAMPARI

1½ OUNCES BEEFEATER LONDON DRY GIN

1 OUNCE PLYMOUTH SLOE GIN

GARNISH: 1 FRESH RASPBERRY

In a mixing glass, gently muddle the raspberry with the Campari. Add ice and the Beefeater and sloe gins, stir, then strain into a chilled cocktail glass. Garnish with the raspberry.

THE MRS. ROBINSON
OF COCKTAILS

———

"The Negroni is the favorite classic cocktail of almost anyone who works in a bar. It's said that every bartender eventually has an affair with the Negroni. The reason for this is that it takes young bartenders down a path from which they will never return. It is the Mrs. Robinson of cocktails: stunning, sexy, and mature. Its dark, alluring color is only a preview for the bittersweet aromas that expand on the palate."

—DUSHAN ZARIC, the 86 Co.

KNICKRONI

FREDERIC YARM, *COCKTAIL VIRGIN SLUT* BLOG, SOMERVILLE, MASSACHUSETTS

Fred, who is a concept cocktailian, explained this drink's origins thusly: "Ever since John Gertsen, who was at No. 9 Park in Boston at the time, told me about his intrigue with the Knickebein, Leo Engel's nineteenth-century pousse-café with an unbroken egg yolk in the middle, I have taken to the drink as a good rite of passage. With the autumnal leaf change coming on, I was thinking about red and yellow drinks, and the vision of a strange merger of a Negroni and a Knickebein occurred. The idea of changing around Leo's recipe was spawned a while ago from the fact that his version's liqueur choices don't hold up to the modern palate, but the Negroni seemed fitting for the fall color theme. I was quite pleased with the results."

½ OUNCE SWEET VERMOUTH

½ OUNCE CAMPARI

1 SMALL OR MEDIUM EGG, SEPARATED, WITH THE YOLK UNBROKEN

½ OUNCE GIN

GARNISH: 1 DASH REGANS' ORANGE BITTERS NO. 6

Stir the vermouth and Campari together in a 2-ounce sherry glass. Gently layer the unbroken egg yolk on top, then carefully layer the gin atop the yolk. Beat the egg white until stiff with a whisk or in a cobbler shaker with a balled-up Hawthorne spring, then cover the gin layer with the egg white. Garnish with the bitters.

THE PROPER PROCEDURE FOR ENJOYING
A KNICKEBEIN-INSPIRED COCKTAIL

It is highly recommended that you drink the Knickroni (page 73), and all such Knickebein-inspired drinks, in the ceremonial four-step process laid out by Leo Engel in 1878:

1. Pass the glass under the *Nostrils* and *Inhale* the *Flavour.*—Pause.

2. Hold the glass *perpendicularly*, close under your mouth, open it *wide*, and suck the froth by drawing a *Deep Breath.*—Pause again.

3. *Point* the lips and take *one-third* of the *liquid contents* remaining in the glass without *touching* the *yolk.*—Pause once more.

4. Straighten the body, throw the *head backward,* swallow the contents remaining in the glass *all at once*, at the same time *breaking the yolk* in your mouth.

BITTERSWEET SYMPHONY

JEFFREY MORGENTHALER, BAR MANAGER, CLYDE COMMON, PORTLAND, OREGON

Cocktails are often referred to as "symphonies in a glass," and this one is, indeed, bittersweet. Jeffrey's creative juices rise well above sea level in this relatively simple drink. Jeffrey, I promise to recognize you next time we meet!

1½ OUNCES LONDON DRY GIN

¾ OUNCE PUNT E MES

¾ OUNCE APEROL

GARNISH: 1 GENEROUS LEMON TWIST

Stir all the ingredients with cracked ice in a mixing glass, then strain into a chilled cocktail glass. Garnish with the lemon twist.

FRENCH NEGRONI

LUDOVIC MIAZGA, GLOBAL AMBASSADOR FOR FRENCH BRANDS,
BACARDI, LTD., LONDON

Ludovic provided the following backstory for this elegant, orange-scented libation: "The French Negroni is a twist on my favorite aperitif cocktail. Instead of using gin, I use Grey Goose L'Orange (inspired by the garnish of a classic Negroni), along with Noilly Prat sweet vermouth and Amer Picon (a great substitute for Campari). I serve it in a rocks glass, but the original was created in France, in Cognac (the home of Grey Goose), and was prepared in a cognac snifter and garnished with a wedge of blood orange. I sometimes like to use a grapefruit twist for enhanced citrus fragrance. In terms of measurements, this is my favorite recipe, but of course it can be made with equal parts of all three spirits or adjusted depending on whether the drinker wishes it to be more bitter, sweet, orangey, and so on."

1 OUNCE GREY GOOSE
L'ORANGE VODKA

⅔ OUNCE AMER PICON

⅚ OUNCE (ABOUT 1 TABLESPOON
PLUS 2 TEASPOONS) NOILLY
PRAT SWEET VERMOUTH

Stir all the ingredients with ice in an old-fashioned glass.

BRAZILEVARDIER

MATTY DURGIN, GREEN RUSSELL BAR, DENVER, COLORADO

Here's how Matty describes this refreshing quaff: "The earthy flavor of the cachaça, the rhubarb and bitter-orange notes of the Aperol, and the vermouth all swim in harmony, and the fresh sugarcane finish from the cachaça rounds things off ever so soundly. I give it a good long stir (20 seconds or so) and then decant from about 24 inches above the cocktail glass to aerate."

1 OUNCE BOCA LOCA CACHAÇA

1 OUNCE PUNT E MES

1 OUNCE APEROL

1 DASH REGANS' ORANGE BITTERS NO. 6

GARNISH: 1 ORANGE TWIST

Stir all the ingredients with cracked ice in a mixing glass, then strain from a height of 24 inches into a chilled cocktail glass. Garnish with the orange twist.

CARICATURE COCKTAIL

GAZ REGAN

This drink is actually a rip-off of a drink called the Old Flame, created by
Dale DeGroff. I played around with Dale's formula a little, then named the
drink in honor of Dale's wife, Jill DeGroff, a graphic artist who executes
fabulous caricatures of the world's leading cocktailian bartenders.

1½ OUNCES GIN	¾ OUNCE COINTREAU
½ OUNCE SWEET VERMOUTH	½ OUNCE FRESH GRAPEFRUIT JUICE
½ OUNCE CAMPARI	GARNISH: 1 ORANGE TWIST

Shake all the ingredients with ice, then strain into a chilled cocktail
glass. Garnish with the orange twist.

DRUNK UNCLE, PAGE 50

WHEN YOU MAKE A NEGRONI,
DON'T FORGET TO DUCK AND PRAY

"The Negroni I enjoy making for myself includes the juice of a wedge of orange and a couple of dashes of orange bitters. When I stir it, I use a lifting motion because the spirits have different weights. Gin is the lightest one, and by lifting as you stir you ensure that all the ingredients are well mixed.

The Negroni was my very first experience of getting a slap from my teacher and mentor Signor Raffaello. I was twelve years old and cocky; I thought that I could make a Negroni without a problem. When he tasted it, he slapped me because it was not balanced. From then on I made sure that every time I was mixing a Negroni, I did two things: duck and pray!"

—SALVATORE CALABRESE, the Playboy Club, London

DOG AND PONY

JILL SAUNDERS, BRAND AMBASSADOR FOR TANQUERAY, PARIS

This Negroni variation has literary origins, as Jill explains: "I created this drink, a twist on both the Negroni and the Dog's Nose cocktail, which is mentioned in Charles Dickens's *Pickwick Papers*, as a tribute to Mr. Walker, the character in the *Pickwick Papers* who lost the use of his right hand after drinking too many Dog's Noses. He became a member of the Brick Lane Temperance Society in East London, so with that in mind, this is my cockney version of the Negroni (Dog and Pony in rhyming slang). I like to think that if Walker had ever changed his mind about the whole Temperance thing and Campari had been around back then, he might have ordered this down at his local gin palace."

1½ OUNCES TANQUERAY NO. TEN GIN

⅔ OUNCE CHOCOLATE PORTER REDUCTION (RECIPE FOLLOWS)

½ OUNCE CAMPARI

GARNISH: 1 ORANGE TWIST

Fill a small beer glass with ice, add all the ingredients, and stir. Garnish with the orange twist.

———

CHOCOLATE PORTER REDUCTION

5 TABLESPOONS SUPERFINE SUGAR   **12 OUNCES CHOCOLATE PORTER**

Combine the sugar and porter in a medium saucepan over medium heat. (Jill uses chocolate porter from London's Meantime Brewing Company.) Bring to a simmer, then lower the heat and simmer gently for 5 minutes. Let cool before using.

BRIDGETOWN STOMP

JULIE REINER, CLOVER CLUB AND FLATIRON LOUNGE, NEW YORK CITY

According to Julie, this Negroni was created on a whim a while ago when she was working at Lani Kai, her New York tiki club that has since closed. Apparently mixology consultant Toby Maloney dropped in to see Julie, and he asked her to make him whatever she liked. This drink became her house Negroni—and it was one of the most popular boozy drinks on the menu. To make the Demerara syrup, simply combine equal parts, by volume, of water and Demerara sugar; heat and stir until the sugar dissolves and allow it to cool to room temperature. Keep in the refrigerator.

2 OUNCES COCKSPUR 12-YEAR RUM

½ OUNCE CINZANO SWEET VERMOUTH

¼ OUNCE CAMPARI

¾ TEASPOON AMARO CIOCIARO

¾ TEASPOON DEMERARA SYRUP (SEE HEADNOTE)

2 DASHES REGANS' ORANGE BITTERS NO. 6

GARNISH: 1 ORANGE TWIST

Stir all the ingredients with ice in a mixing glass, then strain into a chilled old-fashioned glass filled with ice. Garnish with the orange twist.

STREET & SMITH

KATIE STIPE, NEW YORK CITY

Katie says, "I created this drink at Clover Club because I really wanted a cocktail with mezcal on the menu. I was also working with Phil Ward over at newly opened Mayahuel, where the cocktail menu is entirely made up of agave-based drinks. I could see guests' excitement over this mysterious spirit of smoke and earth, and I knew that mezcal was really going places."

1½ OUNCES BLANCO TEQUILA

½ OUNCE MEZCAL

½ OUNCE PUNT E MES

¼ OUNCE CAMPARI INFUSED WITH GRAPEFRUIT PEEL (RECIPE FOLLOWS)

¾ TEASPOON LUXARDO MARASCHINO LIQUEUR

Stir all the ingredients with ice in a mixing glass, then strain into a double old-fashioned glass over 1 big, sexy ice cube.

CAMPARI INFUSED WITH GRAPEFRUIT PEEL

1 LARGE GRAPEFRUIT   **1 (750 ML) BOTTLE CAMPARI**

Use a fine grater to remove the zest from the grapefruit. Combine the zest and Campari in a jar with a tight-fitting lid. Seal the jar and shake gently. Let infuse for about 24 hours. Strain through a double layer of dampened cheesecloth. Store in the refrigerator.

There's a lot to love in my line of work, but if I made a list of my very favorite things in the bar business, mezcal would be close to the top, and the Negroni would be right up there, too.

The Negroni, like so many of its three-ingredient classic drink brethren, is a great litmus test of an unfamiliar bar and bartender: *How long has that sweet vermouth been sitting on the speed rail? Did you ask me what gin? Are you assuming equal parts, or are you throwing tons of booze, which I may not want or need, into my aperitif?* For a simple three-ingredient drink, there sure are an awful lot of ways to screw it up. Simply asking a few questions can ensure that I'm getting exactly what I want. And if I do, that will leave me feeling like I'm in good hands and likely to trust the bartender with another cocktail. But if the bartender tosses in a jigger of vinegar or shakes the life out of it, I'll stick with beer or wine from then on.

And just as a James Brown song wouldn't be the same without a blood-curdling shriek or two, a great mezcal is defined by its earthy, funky, sweaty, dirty, smoky, salty, vegetal weirdness. By "weirdness," I of course mean "deliciousness." It's an acquired taste to be sure, but as with so many of those, it's worth acquiring. I always knew I liked mezcal, and there's something elusive about it that makes me want to keep learning more.

It's true that we bartenders have a tendency to overly fetishize weird ingredients [cough]. Fernet [cough] and certain mezcals can be kind of intimidating to someone used to smooth añejo tequilas, so that works in its favor among too-cool-for-school bartenders. But I think I just fell in love with it because it's a spirit that speaks so clearly and truly about exactly where it comes from and doesn't apologize for one bit of it.

To me, it made a lot of sense to combine these two things I love so much: mezcal and Negronis. The bridge came from a visiting Norwegian bartender, Halvor Digernes, who showed me a brilliant infusion he's been making at his Oslo bar, café, and furniture store(!), Fuglen. He combines Thai bird's-eye chiles, roasted coffee beans, and Campari and lets that sit for a while. I've continued to play with the infusion and settled on one comprised of 22 grams each of dried morita, mulato, and bird's-eye chiles and 8 teaspoons of freshly roasted coffee beans in 1 liter of Campari. I let it sit for about three hours, then strain and refrigerate. The savory coffee notes offset Campari's inherent sweetness, and the heat from the chiles takes some of your palate's attention away from Campari's characteristic bitterness.

The Negroni variation I make with this infusion is the Mañanita, a slightly top-heavy mezcal Negroni. It consists of 1 ounce of an equal-parts blend of Punt e Mes and Dolin rouge (our house sweet vermouth spec at Death & Co), 1 ounce of the infused Campari, and 1½ ounces of your mezcal of choice. I think Sombra and Del Maguey Vida are both excellent in this drink, as well as remarkably affordable mixing spirits. Then just stir briefly and strain over fresh ice in a rocks glass. Top it with an expressed orange peel and take a cautionary sip. It will bite you back, but you like that, don't you?

—Joaquín Simó, partner and bartender, Pouring Ribbons,
New York City

NEGRONI HORS PAIR

COLIN PETER FIELD, THE HEMINGWAY BAR AT THE RITZ, PARIS

Before I turn you over to Colin, I should tell you that the recipe below was created by a bartender in Germany whose name we don't know, and that the name of this drink, Negroni Hors Pair (the Peerless Negroni), is something I conjured up after reading Colin's account below. Okay, over to Colin.

"I was recently judging a marvelous competition sponsored by Campari in Munich. Mauro Mahjoub from Mauro's Negroni Club (see page 64) was the host, along with the incredible Charles Schumann, who was a host one evening. Mahjoub's new bar is very large, and his bartenders are loaded with professionalism. The atmosphere was stupendous.

"One young lady, who hardly trembled as she displayed her talent *hors pair* [peerless talent] completely seduced me with her Negroni recipe. I wish that I trembled so little in competitions, and I wish that I had invented this cocktail. I also wish that I had written down her name, but I hope that she reads this and spontaneously manifests herself to us. She didn't win the competition, but her cocktail was the one that inspired me the most. I was enthralled by the taste and its mysterious darkness, which seems to befit Comte Negroni's cocktail . . . The young woman saw how much I loved her cocktail and offered me a bottle of 15-year-old balsamic vinegar. I'm almost sure that I will never see her again, but I will always remember the few minutes that I passed with her and her cocktail. For that matter, I don't even remember the name of the cocktail, perhaps because this was the *real* Negroni."

1 OUNCE BEEFEATER 24 GIN

1 OUNCE TAYLOR FLADGATE
20-YEAR PORT

1 OUNCE CAMPARI

4 DASHES 15-YEAR BALSAMIC
VINEGAR MADE FROM PEDRO
XIMENEZ GRAPES

GARNISH: 1 ORANGE WHEEL AND
1 SQUARE PIECE OF LEMON ZEST

Stir all the ingredients with ice in a tumbler. Garnish with the orange wheel and lemon zest.

"IF THEY MADE NEGRONI TOOTHPASTE, I'D USE IT."

—NAREN YOUNG, Saxon + Parole, New York City

WHEN I GREW UP

"If a person could model oneself after a cocktail, I knew that the Negroni was exactly what I wanted to be when I grew up."

—MICHAEL PROCOPIO, *Food for the Thoughtless* blog

UNCLE NEGRONI

MICHELE FIORDOLIVA, NEGRONI BAR, MUNICH

Michele says, "Because we have lot of American guests [at the Negroni Bar], I thought about making a Negroni to please the American palate. Then of course I needed a good American ingredient: bourbon." This is a great post-prandial potion.

²/₃ OUNCE ELIJAH CRAIG 12-YEAR BOURBON

1 OUNCE CARPANO ANTICA FORMULA VERMOUTH

³/₄ OUNCE CAMPARI

½ OUNCE CYNAR

2 DASHES BITTERMENS XOCOLATL MOLE BITTERS

GARNISH: 1 SLICE OF DRIED ORANGE

Stir all the ingredients with ice in a double old-fashioned glass. Garnish with the dried orange slice.

BUÑUELONI

JEFF "BEACHBUM" BERRY, AUTHOR OF SIX BOOKS ON EXOTIC COCKTAILS AND
CUISINE, THE LATEST BEING *BEACHBUM BERRY'S POTIONS OF THE CARIBBEAN:
500 YEARS OF TROPICAL DRINKS AND THE PEOPLE BEHIND THEM*

Jeff provided an intriguing account of the origins of this drink: "It was created in about 1954 by one of my favorite film directors, Luis Buñuel (*Un Chien Andalou, The Discreet Charm of the Bourgeoisie*). He once dared actor Jaime Fernandez, 'If you drink four of these, I'll give you a film.' Fernandez had to admit defeat after two. Buñuel's producer Serge Silberman gave the recipe to Buñuel biographer John Baxter in the 1990s, and I tweaked it slightly to create this version."

2¼ OUNCES BEEFEATER
LONDON DRY GIN

1 OUNCE SWEET VERMOUTH

¾ OUNCE PUNT E MES

GARNISH: 1 ORANGE WEDGE

Shake all the ingredients with ice, then strain into a rocks glass packed with crushed ice. Garnish with the orange wedge.

GAIJIN

KIRSTI KINSERVIK, ALEXANDER VALLEY BAR, HEALDSBURG, CALIFORNIA

Gaijin means "foreigner" in Japanese, and this Negroni variation makes great use of one of the fine whiskeys that country is producing these days.

1½ OUNCES AKASHI WHITE OAK BLENDED WHISKEY

1 OUNCE BIGALLET "CHINA-CHINA" AMER LIQUEUR

1 OUNCE CAMPARI

1 DASH REGANS' ORANGE BITTERS NO. 6

GARNISH: 1 ORANGE TWIST

Stir all the ingredients with ice in a mixing glass, then strain into a chilled coupe. Garnish with the orange twist.

MELA D'ALBA

ANDREW FRIEDMAN, LIBERTY, SEATTLE

Here's what Andrew has to say about how he fortuitously stumbled upon this creation: "This is a *delicious* variant of the Negroni. I made it by accident when I was reaching for the Rittenhouse rye to make a variant in and of itself of the Boulevardier but mistakenly grabbed the Laird's next to it. I measured, mixed, and stirred it, then gave it a taste and realized that something was different—wonderfully different. This is one of those drinks with a combination of spirits that creates a whole new flavor."

2 OUNCES LAIRD'S BONDED APPLE BRANDY

1 OUNCE SWEET VERMOUTH

1 OUNCE CAMPARI

GARNISH: 1 LEMON TWIST

Stir all the ingredients with ice in a double old-fashioned glass. Garnish with the lemon twist.

MY FAVE!

MOSES LABOY, RED ROOSTER, NEW YORK CITY

Moses is justifiably enthused about his sophisticated Negroni variation: "My play on the Negroni is hands down my favorite cocktail: sweet, bitter, and boozy all in one glass!"

1½ OUNCES BULLEIT BOURBON INFUSED WITH SKILLET-ROASTED FIGS AND PEARS (RECIPE FOLLOWS)

1 OUNCE DOLIN SWEET VERMOUTH

1 OUNCE CAMPARI

GARNISH: 1 ROASTED FIG (PREPARED AS IN THE RECIPE THAT FOLLOWS)

Stir all the ingredients with ice in a mixing glass, then strain into a chilled cocktail glass. Garnish with the fig and behold your guests' enjoyment!

———

BULLEIT BOURBON INFUSED WITH SKILLET-ROASTED FIGS AND PEARS

2 ANJOU PEARS, QUARTERED

8 FIGS, HALVED

5 OUNCES WATER

1 LITER BULLEIT BOURBON

Preheat the oven to 350° Fahrenheit. Heat a dry cast-iron skillet over high heat until very hot. Put the pears and the figs in the skillet and stir until the figs begin to blister. Pour the water over the fruit, stir, and then transfer the skillet to the oven. Bake for 12 minutes.

Transfer the contents of the skillet to a sturdy heatproof jar, pour in the bourbon, and seal the jar. Shake the jar gently once or twice a day for 2 days. Strain through a double layer of dampened cheesecloth.

ALEXANDRIA HOTEL COCKTAIL,
AKA SPRING STREET DISTRICT COCKTAIL

MARCOS TELLO, THE VARNISH, LOS ANGELES

This cocktail, created by the fabulous Marcos Tello of Los Angeles, was brought to this book courtesy of Ted Munat, author of *Left Coast Libations*. The drink uses cachaça, a sugar-based Brazilian spirit that can be thought of as a style of rum, but Ted notes that "this isn't your stereotypical muddled fruit and lime juice cachaça drink. The Alexandria Hotel Cocktail first saw light of day in 2009, when Marcos helped to put together the Los Angeles Sub-District Cocktail Competition. His idea was to emulate New York City, which early on had the Manhattan, Bronx, and Brooklyn cocktails, then later the Red Hook, Greenpoint, Little Italy, Bensonhurst, and so on. Marcos even went so far as to emulate the style of these signature New York City drinks, making it a rule of the competition that the drinks must be stirred cocktails made using a base spirit, modifying vermouth, liqueur or a sweetening agent, and some type of bitters, without citrus, homemade ingredients, or extremely obscure, hard-to-find ingredients."

The old Alexandria Hotel was an iconic Los Angeles spot and, according to Tello, "a magnet for old, glamorous Hollywood. Even the carpet was called 'the million dollar carpet,' because it was said that a million dollars in business was done there every day."

1 OUNCE SILVER CACHAÇA

1 OUNCE CAMPARI

½ OUNCE MATHILDE PEACH LIQUEUR

1 DASH FEE BROTHERS WEST INDIAN ORANGE BITTERS

1 DASH REGANS' ORANGE BITTERS NO. 6

GARNISH: 1 ORANGE TWIST

Stir all the ingredients with ice in a mixing glass, then strain into a chilled cocktail glass. Flame the orange twist over the drink, then discard.

CAMILLO IN XELA

MAX LA ROCCA, HOST OF THE POPULAR MIXOLOGY BLOG *LISTEN TO THE ICE*

Max, one of my favorite bartenders—we go back a few years at this point—told me the following about his Negroni variation: "The drink I made for this precious little book is called Camillo in Xela, Xela being the indigenous name for Quetzaltenango, the city in Guatemala where the House of Zacapa is located. The rum used in this recipe is aged at over 7,500 feet in elevation. Of course you all know who Camillo is . . .

"Being from Italy, where coffee is a very important element of the culture, I was curious to play with the toasted flavor of this amazing ingredient. It echoes the bitterness of the Campari and complements the complexity of the Carpano Antica Formula and the beautiful hints of vanilla, almond, and chocolate of the Zacapa 23. The coffee is also fitting, given that the Zacapa comes from Guatemala, one of the world's leading producers of coffee."

8 COFFEE BEANS

1 OUNCE ZACAPA 23-YEAR RUM

¾ OUNCE CARPANO ANTICA FORMULA

½ OUNCE CAMPARI

GARNISH: 1 LONG ORANGE TWIST

Flame the coffee beans with a blowtorch. Put 5 of them in a mixing glass and crush them with the flat end of a barspoon. Add the remaining ingredients and stir without ice for 30 seconds. Add ice, stir, then double strain into a double old-fashioned glass filled with ice. Garnish with the orange twist and the 3 remaining coffee beans.

PEPPER NEGRONI

JASON WALSH, MIXOLOGIST AND BAR CONSULTANT, NEW YORK CITY

The genius in this cocktail lies in the serrano-infused Chartreuse—it's an inspired touch—but I strongly advise that you taste the infusion after 12 hours, then every 2 hours after that, straining the mixture before the chiles take over the liqueur. Just trust your senses on this.

1 OUNCE PLYMOUTH GIN

1 OUNCE DOLIN SWEET VERMOUTH

1 OUNCE YELLOW CHARTREUSE INFUSED WITH SERRANOS (RECIPE FOLLOWS)

GARNISH: 1 ORANGE TWIST AND 1 SLICE CHILE PEPPER

Stir all the ingredients with ice in a mixing glass, then strain into a chilled coupe. Garnish with the orange twist and slice of chile pepper.

———

YELLOW CHARTREUSE INFUSED WITH SERRANOS

3 SERRANO CHILES, SPLIT LENGTHWISE

1 (750 ML) BOTTLE YELLOW CHARTREUSE

Combine the serranos and Chartreuse in a jar with a tight-fitting lid. Seal the jar and shake gently. Let infuse for about 24 hours. Strain through a double layer of dampened cheesecloth.

ONCE YOU FALL FOR THE NEGRONI

"I am in the camp of people who love the Negroni and believe the world wouldn't be complete without it. I've always compared the Negroni to a pint of Guinness. The first pint of Guinness you ever drink tastes a little too bitter, but if you make it to a third pint, you'll be drinking it for the rest of your life. I feel the same way about the Negroni. The first one appeals only to those that have already acquired a taste for bitters, but once you fall for the Negroni, you will drink it for the rest of your life."

—SIMON FORD, the 86 Company

D.O.M.E. NEGRONI

MIHAI FETCU, ROMANIA

Mihai is one of the most prominent bartenders in Romania, a country that seems to have way more cocktailian genii than you might think. Mihai's use of genever in this drink is inspired—it takes the heavy vanilla edge off the Carpano Antica Formula, and it also play nice with the rest of the ingredients.

1 OUNCE BOLS BARREL-AGED
GENEVER

⅓ OUNCE CARPANO
ANTICA FORMULA

⅓ OUNCE MARTINI & ROSSI
SWEET VERMOUTH

⅓ OUNCE DUBONNET ROUGE

1 OUNCE APEROL

1 DASH FEE BROTHERS GIN
BARREL-AGED ORANGE BITTERS

1 DASH REGANS'
ORANGE BITTERS NO. 6

GARNISH: 1 ORANGE TWIST

Stir all the ingredients with ice in a mixing glass, then strain into an old-fashioned glass over a ball of molded ice. Squeeze the orange twist over the drink, then add it as a garnish.

PIZZA NEGRONI

MORGAN SCHICK, TRICK DOG, SAN FRANCISCO

While this cocktail sounds like the invention of a stoned teenager in his parents' basement, in fact it's a deliciously savory, wonderfully refined drink. The Tomato Water recipe makes a little less than 2 cups. *(Pictured on page 110.)*

1 OUNCE AVIATION GIN INFUSED WITH MOZZARELLA AND PARMESAN (RECIPE FOLLOWS)

1 OUNCE MARTINI & ROSSI GRAN LUSSO VERMOUTH

1 OUNCE CAMPARI

½ OUNCE TOMATO WATER (RECIPE FOLLOWS)

LEMON TWIST

GARNISH: 1 OLIVE AND 1 SLICE SALAMI

Stir all the ingredients with ice in a mixing glass for about half as long as you would normally, then strain into a chilled cocktail glass. Squeeze the lemon twist over the drink, then discard. Skewer the olive and salami slice with a cocktail pick, garnish, and serve.

AVIATION GIN INFUSED WITH MOZZARELLA AND PARMESAN

4 OUNCES MOZZARELLA CHEESE, ROUGHLY CHOPPED

2 OUNCES RIND FROM PARMESAN CHEESE, ROUGHLY CHOPPED

1 (750 ML) BOTTLE AVIATION GIN

Combine the mozzarella, parmesan, and gin in a jar with a tight-fitting lid. Seal the jar and shake gently. Let infuse for 5 to 7 days. Discard the solids, then freeze for 24 hours. Strain once more through a coffee filter to remove any solidified fat.

TOMATO WATER

1½ POUNDS RIPE TOMATOES

LARGE PINCH OF SALT

Line a sieve with cheesecloth and set it over a large bowl. Coarsely chop the tomatoes, then place in the lined sieve and sprinkle with salt. Cover and chill for at least 12 hours, then discard the solids and use the tomato water as directed.

PIZZA NEGRONI, PAGE 108

NEGRONIS IN BORNEO AT 4,000 METERS

"I once made a bottled Negroni to take with me when climbing Mount Kinabalu in Borneo. I used equal parts Gordon's gin, Martini Rosso, Campari, and tap water. When we slept in a refuge at 3,000 meters (about 10,000 feet) in elevation, I left the bottle outside to chill. We drank it when we reached the summit, at 4,095 meters. The Negroni was cold as ice. Delicious."

—NICOLAS DE SOTO, London

WHO SAYS THAT PERFECTION CANNOT BE ACHIEVED?

"The Negroni is the only classic Italian cocktail that truly belongs to the international cocktail culture. Without a doubt, Campari and sweet vermouth are to Italy what bourbon is to America! What I love the most is watching first-time Negroni drinkers going after the second sip and getting hooked on this perfectly integrated ambrosia of three liquors. The drink is a true embodiment of sophistication for the palate and simplicity in the making! Here's to those who say that perfection cannot be achieved. *Cin cin salute!*"

—FRANCESCO LAFRANCONI, Southern Wine & Spirits, Las Vegas

NEGRONI DE PROVENCE

NICOLAS DE SOTO, HEAD BARTENDER, EXPERIMENTAL COCKTAIL CLUB, NEW YORK CITY

Nicolas is clearly on board with the concept of this book: "For me, the Negroni is the perfect all-time drink. You can do so many variations using different levels of juniper, bitterness, and sweetness to please different palates. Unless you hate bitterness, it's a drink for everyone."

1¼ OUNCES CITADELLE GIN INFUSED WITH LAVENDER (RECIPE FOLLOWS)

¾ OUNCE LILLET BLANC INFUSED WITH HERBES DE PROVENCE (RECIPE FOLLOWS)

1 OUNCE SALERS GENTIANE APERITIF

Stir all the ingredients with ice in a double old-fashioned glass.

CITADELLE GIN INFUSED WITH LAVENDER

3 OUNCES DRIED LAVENDER   **1 (750 ML) BOTTLE CITADELLE GIN**

Combine the lavender and gin in a jar with a tight-fitting lid. Seal the jar and shake gently. Let infuse for about 8 hours or overnight. Strain through a double layer of dampened cheesecloth.

LILLET BLANC INFUSED WITH HERBES DE PROVENCE

½ CUP HERBES DE PROVENCE   **1 (750 ML) BOTTLE LILLET BLANC**

Combine the herbes de Provence and Lillet in a jar with a tight-fitting lid. Seal the jar and shake gently. Let infuse overnight. Strain through a double layer of dampened cheesecloth.

SOUTHPAW

JOSEPH BOLEY, RED HOUSE, PARIS

According to Joseph, "This is a direct variation of Sam Ross's Left Hand Cocktail, which appeared in Jim Meehan's *PDT Cocktail Book*. The Left Hand is named after Al Pacino's character Lefty Ruggiero in *Donnie Brasco*. I wanted to create a meaner drink to represent the hitman. For the bourbon, my go-to in France, where the selection is limited, is Four Roses single-barrel."

1 OUNCE GOOD BOURBON	1 TEASPOON FERNET-BRANCA
½ OUNCE PUNT E MES	2 DASHES PEYCHAUD'S BITTERS
½ OUNCE CAMPARI	GARNISH: 1 ORANGE TWIST

Stir all the ingredients with ice in a mixing glass, then strain into a chilled cocktail glass. Garnish with the orange twist.

PISCORONI

GAZ REGAN

Right before I put this book to bed, my friend Diego Loret de Mola, from BevMax in Connecticut, sent me a care package that was chockablock full of BarSol pisco, and it also contained a couple of bottles of Perfecto Amor, a fortified wine similar to sherry that gets its kick from a shot of pisco brandy that's added to the base wine before bottling. *Hmm* . . . , I thought. Watch the measurements on this one—Perfecto Amor can be a dominant soul. And *don't* overdo the Angostura! By the way, if you can't find Perfecto Amor in your neck of the woods, you can use amontillado sherry in its stead.

2 OUNCES BARSOL SELECTO
ITALIA PISCO

1 OUNCE NOILLY PRAT
SWEET VERMOUTH

½ OUNCE CAMPARI

1 TEASPOON BARSOL PERFECTO AMOR

1 DASH ANGOSTURA BITTERS

GARNISH: 1 ORANGE TWIST

Stir all the ingredients with ice in a mixing glass, then strain into a double old-fashioned glass over 1 huge rock of ice. Garnish with the orange twist.

POUSSE-PORT NEGRONI

DOMINGO-MARTIN BARRERES, MIXOLOGIST,
MARKET BY JEAN-GEORGES, W HOTEL, BOSTON

Domingo is an artist behind the bar, and he takes his craft very seriously, as you'll discover if you make this drink. He's also a darned good chap to hang at airport bars with. Trust me on this.

1½ OUNCES BOMBAY SAPPHIRE GIN

1½ OUNCES RAMOS PINTO RESERVA PORT

1½ OUNCES CAMPARI

GARNISH: 1 ORANGE SPIRAL MADE WITH A CHANNEL KNIFE

Put the liquors in three individual mixing glasses. Fill the glass containing Campari halfway with ice. Stir for 10 seconds, then strain into a pousse-café glass. Repeat with the port, but strain it over the back of a barspoon to layer the port on top of the Campari. Repeat with the gin, straining it over the spoon as well to float it on top of the port. Garnish with the orange spiral.

STILETTA

PHIL WARD, MAYAHUEL, NEW YORK CITY

Cocktail genius Phil Ward didn't pull any punches when he described this drink's origins: "I was hungover and drinking Campari and soda while doing my chores at the bar. I was mulling cider and putting in the star anise just as I took a sip of Campari. I was like, *Wow, could those two tyrants actually coexist?* I tried it. They did."

1½ OUNCES EL TESORO
BLANCO TEQUILA

1 OUNCE CARPANO ANTICA FORMULA

1 OUNCE CAMPARI INFUSED WITH
STAR ANISE (RECIPE FOLLOWS)

Stir all the ingredients with ice in a mixing glass, then strain into a chilled cocktail glass.

———

CAMPARI INFUSED WITH STAR ANISE

20 STAR ANISE PODS   **1 (750 ML) BOTTLE CAMPARI**

Combine the star anise and Campari in a jar with a tight-fitting lid. Seal the jar and shake gently. Let infuse for about 8 hours or overnight. Strain through a double layer of dampened cheesecloth.

UNUSUAL NEGRONI

CHARLOTTE VOISEY, MIXOLOGIST WITH WILLIAM GRANT & SONS DISTILLERS, USA

Charlotte says, "I like a delicate touch, especially when it comes to Negronis. This variation is a light alternative, great for first timers."

1 OUNCE HENDRICK'S GIN

1 OUNCE LILLET BLANC

1 OUNCE APEROL

GARNISH: 1 SMALL GRAPEFRUIT SLICE OR 1 GRAPEFRUIT TWIST

Stir all the ingredients with ice in a rocks glass, then garnish with the grapefruit slice. Alternatively, stir all the ingredients with ice in a mixing glass, then strain into a chilled cocktail glass and garnish with the grapefruit twist.

ORANGES *ARE* THE ONLY FRUIT, BY ROSIE SCHAAP

Rosie Schaap writes the "Drink" column for the New York Times Magazine *and is the author of the memoir* Drinking with Men, *which came out in January 2013. Rosie wrote this fine essay for the first edition of this book, and I had to include it here.*

I'm one of those bartenders who tells anyone who'll listen: don't listen to anyone. (Even, or especially, me.) Drink what gives you pleasure, I say. Pay Mr. Award-Winning Craft Mixolohistorian no mind. Ignore whatever those well-dressed, glossy-haired, youngish people at stupidly expensive lounges are doing; the sketchy hedge fund they manage will probably go under next season, just as this year's trendiest bottle of booze will collect dust in the back of your pantry before long. As for tradition, it has its place, but we are meant to defy it as our hearts and palates dictate.

So it is with an uneasy mix of pain and pride that I tell you this: I don't mess with the Negroni. The straightforwardness of its customary 1:1:1 proportions is not only elegant, it's also a gift to anyone behind a busy bar who gets even the least bit addled when trying to remember recipes. My own weird mnemonic for the drink, when I still needed such a mechanism, was a robust shout—only in my mind, of course, so as not to alarm the customers—of *equality!*, my cue that the drink demands equal parts gin, sweet vermouth, and Campari.

Oranges, we are reminded by the title of Jeanette Winterson's excellent first novel, are not the only fruit. Except when it comes to the Negroni. In this instance, for me, nothing else will do. Keep your cute Key limes and comely kumquats, your thick-skinned pomelos and beautifully sinister Buddha's hands for other purposes. The Negroni is the orange's domain, and its alone. Some will tell you that the cocktail needs no fruit at all, but this isn't a matter of *need*. Others prefer lemon; here I differ with, for instance, gaz himself. The aromatic oil of a lemon gives off an almost angular sharpness, laced by the faintest sweetness.

The orange does the opposite: first and foremost is that warm, redolent sweetness, with a crisp, acid tang trailing a good way behind it.

If Winterson's protagonist yearned for something less everyday than an orange, the poet Ben Belitt, in "An Orange in Mérida," describes the fruit in terms that are anything but quotidian:

> ... the orange's pith is broken
> in a blind effervescence that perfumes the palate and burns
> to the tooth's bite.
> And the dead reawaken.

In truth, the matter of a Negroni's most suitable garnish didn't seem like such a big, poetry-worthy deal to me, either—not until the evening when a regular at the little Brooklyn neighborhood bar where I work surprised me by ordering the drink. It's mostly a beer-and-shots bar, and beyond margaritas and the occasional call for a martini or a Manhattan, few mixed drinks are ever requested. Sure, we had the gin. The vermouth. The Campari. But no oranges. At this bar, we don't *do* oranges. I explained the situation to the regular and asked, "Okay if I use lemon instead?"

He said it was okay. So I sliced off some lemon peel, spritzed it across the drink's surface, dropped it in, and set the drink before him. As he took a sip, his face twisted up. I could tell that the substitution had upset the balance and disappointed his expectations. A small swatch of orange peel and a spray of its essence might seem to do little to enhance or in any substantial way alter the character of the cocktail. But it makes a big difference. It really does.

My regular's a good sport, though, and not one to let otherwise perfectly good liquor go to waste. He wasn't satisfied with his Negroni that night, but he drank it down. And even now, when the mood strikes him, he'll still order one. But he knows to come prepared—with an orange in his pocket.

the Large Format Negronis

Here we look at some recipes for what bartenders know as batch cocktails. This merely means that the drinks are premixed in large quantities, which makes them ideal if you're going to throw a party and don't want to spend all of your time making individual drinks for everyone. Some of the drinks in this chapter need to be prepared well in advance of serving—a matter of weeks, not hours—so be sure to read the recipe thoroughly before starting out on what could be a fabulous escapade into large-format Negronis.

I should also mention that almost all of the recipes in the previous chapter can be made into large-format Negronis. Simply multiply the ingredients by whatever number suits your need and store them in bottles or pitchers. When it's time to serve, add ice or pour into ice-filled old-fashioned glasses, adding garnishes as appropriate.

BOTTLE-AGED AND VINT-AGED NEGRONIS

TONY CONIGLIARO, 69 COLEBROOKE ROW, LONDON

Tony is one of the world's preeminent bartenders, and the man behind 69 Colebrooke Row—a fantastic, wildly inventive bar in London's Islington neighborhood. Tony is known for doing weird and wonderful things with cocktails—including using tools and techniques from molecular gastronomy, like Rotavapors and sous-vide machines, to create custom ingredients.

But for all his technological wizardry, Tony still loves a good classic. He says, "I love Negronis because to me they are the signifier for *aperitivo*. As an Italian, I so appreciate that as a cultural concept. The *aperitivo* says, *Work is over. It's time to open your palate and start to enjoy your night!* But being me, I couldn't just let the Negroni be a Negroni! I wanted to see what else I could do with it—what other directions it could take.

"I first started aging Negronis five years ago. We had great success with Manhattans and wanted to see what else we could use the process with. When you age a cocktail, it mellows considerably; the different spirits combine on a molecular level and come together beautifully. We started flash-fusing ingredients for the Negroni in the sous-vide to see if we could approximate the effect of aging without the time commitment. We experimented with periods between one and twenty-four hours.

"We found that the longer you cooked it, the more it tasted like it had been aged in the bottle for a long time. We started serving these 'vint-aged' Negronis at the bar, and they were a great hit. It was fantastic to discover something that created the effect of aging without having to stick a lot of bottles in the cellar!"

CONTINUED

Few people have access to sous-vide machines, and I'm not one of the few, so instead of flash-fusing (combining the three ingredients, vacuum-sealing them in a bag, and dropping it into a sous-vide machine for a certain amount of time), I allow my vint-aged Negronis to mature slowly, in bottles. It takes longer, but you get there in the end.

The bottled Negronis make great favors to take to parties. When you open and serve them—over ice in a double old-fashioned glass—be sure to have some freshly cut orange twists handy for garnishes.

MAKES 76 OUNCES; SERVES ABOUT 25

1 (750 ML) BOTTLE GIN

1 (750 ML) BOTTLE CAMPARI

1 (750 ML) BOTTLE SWEET VERMOUTH

Stir all the ingredients together in a large container. Decant into smaller bottles. (I like to reuse and relabel the original gin, vermouth, and Campari bottles.) Store out of direct sunlight for at least 1 month, at which point subtle changes in flavor should be detectable. In theory, you could age these Negronis indefinitely, but chances are you won't. Six months of aging makes an incredible difference, and to be honest, I've never managed to store my Negronis any longer than that.

BARREL-AGED NEGRONIS

JEFFREY MORGENTHALER, BAR MANAGER, CLYDE COMMON, PORTLAND, OREGON

Jeffrey has been, and continues to be, a leading force in the twenty-first-century bartending and cocktailian movement. He visited Tony Conigliaro at 69 Colebrooke Row in London in 2010 and, inspired by Conigliaro's Manhattans aged in glass vessels, he returned to Portland to try his hand at barrel-aged cocktails, which he calls "a decidedly American curiosity."

On his popular, eponymous blog, Jeffrey Morgenthaler discusses his approach: "The rub of aging cocktails in a glass bottle is that the whole premise is built upon subtlety, as we know that spirits aged in glass or steel do so at an unremarkable pace. Being from the United States, where—as everyone is aware—bigger equals better, I pondered the following question: What if you could prepare a large batch of a single, spirit-driven cocktail and age it in a used oak barrel?

"A hundred some-odd dollars in liquor later, I was nervously pouring a gallon of pre-batched rye Manhattans into a small, used oak cask whose previous contents were Madeira wine. I plugged the barrel and sat back in anxious anticipation. If the experiment was a success, I'd have a delicious cocktail to share at the bar; if it was a failure, then I'd be pouring the restaurant's money down the floor drain.

"Over the next several weeks I popped open the barrel to test my little concoction until I stumbled upon the magic mark at five to six weeks. And there it was, lying beautifully on the finish: a soft blend of oak, wine, caramel, and char. That first batch sold out in a matter of days, and I was left with a compelling need to push the process even further."

CONTINUED

Morgenthaler's Manhattan project was a success, and he soon moved on to Negronis: "After six weeks in the bourbon barrel, our Negroni emerged a rare beauty: the sweet vermouth so slightly oxidized, the color paler and rosier than the original, the mid-palate softly mingled with whiskey, the finish long and lingering with oak tannins. We knew we were onto something unique and immediately made plans to take the cask-aging program to the next level."

Now even home bartenders are exploring barrel aging, benefiting from the fact that it's quite easy to order used (or new) oak barrels online. One reliable source for used whiskey barrels is the online store at Tuthilltown Spirits in New York. They sell 3-gallon charred oak barrels that were previously used for whiskey. Three gallons yields about 128 drinks—perfect for a large party, a wedding, or a particularly boozy family reunion. Morgenthaler decants his cocktails into glass vessels. However, you can also drill a hole into the side of the barrel and insert a spigot; any home brew, wine-making, or vinegar-making shop should supply spigots, and they might even drill the hole for you.

MAKES ABOUT 3 GALLONS; SERVES ABOUT 128

5 (750 ML) BOTTLES DRY GIN	**5 (750 ML) BOTTLES CAMPARI**
5 (750 ML) BOTTLES SWEET VERMOUTH	

Stir all the ingredients together in a large container. Pour into a 3-gallon oak barrel and let rest for 5 to 7 weeks. Decant into glass bottles until ready to serve.

GFE NEGRONI

JIM GEURTS, TRIPLE J. BAR, BILZEN, BELGIUM

This drink is named for Don Julio González-Frausto Estrada, the founder of Don Julio tequila. Jim Geurts recommends that you allow the bottled cocktail to rest for at least a few days, preferably a week, before serving. He notes that he once allowed a bottle to age for eight months and says, "The flavors keep changing."

MAKES ABOUT 23 OUNCES; SERVES ABOUT 7

6 OUNCES DON JULIO REPOSADO TEQUILA

5½ OUNCES CARPANO ANTICA FORMULA VERMOUTH

6½ OUNCES CAMPARI

5 OUNCES MINERAL WATER

10 DASHES PEYCHAUD'S BITTERS

10 DASHES ANGOSTURA BITTERS

GARNISH: ORANGE TWISTS

Pour all the ingredients into a 1-liter bottle and refrigerate for at least a few days. Serve over ice in old-fashioned glasses, garnished with freshly cut orange twists.

CRAVING THE BITTERSWEET TASTE

"The Negroni was one of the first cocktails that I learned to make. I'm pretty sure my first one was when I was seventeen or eighteen and was making dinner from the *Joy of Cooking* cookbook. The cocktails in the front section fascinated me, and I knew that my parents had a crusty bottle of Campari from the sixties hanging out on the bar. My mom always cooked with sweet vermouth (Julia Child said it was okay), and gin and tonics were a regular summer pastime. Curious as I was, I made a small Negroni just to see what it was like.

"It was not love at first sight. I figured that there had to be a reason it was included in the book, as they seemed to be very selective about the recipes they chose to include. So I sipped on it while making dinner. The medicinal qualities mellowed as the ice melted, and toward the end of the first time I had it, I wasn't hooked, but I noticed myself craving the bittersweet taste of the cocktail.

"As a professional bartender, the Negroni is one of the cocktails I find myself returning to when looking for something to serve as an aperitif to guests before dinner. It's also one of those cocktails that I feel comfortable ordering pretty much anywhere. If I'm at a bar and spy a bottle of Campari, there's a good chance that I'll order a Negroni if the mood strikes."

—KEVIN BURKE, head barman, Colt & Gray,
Denver, Colorado

STRAWBERRY NEGRONI

JARED BROWN AND ANISTATIA MILLER, MIXELLANY, LTD., LONDON

Jared and Anistatia are very good friends of mine, and although the attribution above suggests that they live in London, they actually dwell in the picturesque English countryside. Should you ever be lucky enough to visit them there, this is the sort of top-notch yet very simple treat you can expect to enjoy.

MAKES ABOUT 18 OUNCES; SERVES ABOUT 6

6 OUNCES SIPSMITH V.J.O.P. GIN

6 OUNCES SWEET VERMOUTH

6 OUNCES CAMPARI

8 LARGE STRAWBERRIES, VERY THINLY SLICED

Stir all the ingredients together in a large glass pitcher—the prettiest one you can find. Let sit for at least 10 minutes to infuse the cocktail with the flavor of the strawberries. Add ice, stir, and serve.

BLACKBERRY BITTER

DANI TATARIN, KEEFER BAR, VANCOUVER, BRITISH COLUMBIA

This punch is ideal for summertime parties. The orange zest really makes it come alive, and the blackberry garnishes are a special treat.

MAKES ABOUT 100 OUNCES; SERVES ABOUT 33

1 LITER PLYMOUTH GIN

1 LITER MARTINI BIANCO

1 LITER CAMPARI

48 FRESH BLACKBERRIES

ZEST OF 2 ORANGES

SIMPLE SYRUP (1:1 SUGAR:WATER)

Stir the gin, Martini Bianco, Campari, blackberries, and orange zest together in a large container. Refrigerate for at least 3 days and up to 2 months. Strain through a double layer of dampened cheesecloth, reserving the blackberries. Pour the cocktail into bottles and store in the refrigerator. Put the blackberries in a container and add enough simple syrup to cover them. Store the blackberries in the refrigerator as well.

To serve, transfer to ice-filled pitchers or a punch bowl, or pour into ice-filled old-fashioned glasses. Garnish each cocktail with a blackberry on a cocktail pick.

the Edible Negronis

Edible drinks ain't new—they go all the way back to the mid-1800s, if not further. In 1862, bartender Jerry Thomas published the world's very first cocktail recipe book, *How to Mix Drinks; or, The Bon-Vivant's Companion*, which among bartenders is commonly referred to as "the 1862 book." Within its pages, Thomas details a recipe for Punch Jelly, a drink that was nothing more, and nothing less, than a punch with added isinglass, a form of gelatin obtained from fish bladders. The punch is then poured into molds and allowed to set. This jelly was rather potent, though, so Thomas warns readers, "This preparation is a very agreeable refreshment on a cold night, but should be used in moderation . . . many persons, particularly of the softer sex, have been tempted to partake so plentifully of it as to render them somewhat unfit for waltzing or quadrilling after supper."

It's doubtful that any of the following edible Negroni recipes will hinder your dancing skills, and it's fabulous to see just how creative people can be in displaying their talents by creating all manner of cocktail-related comestibles for your delight.

NEGRONI POPSICLE

JAKE GODBY, CHEF AND OWNER, HUMPHRY SLOCOMBE ICE CREAM,
SAN FRANCISCO

What could be more refreshing than walking around on a hot summer's day with one of these to keep your mouth watering, huh?

MAKES ABOUT 12 POPSICLES, DEPENDING ON THE SIZE OF YOUR MOLD

1 CUP WATER

½ CUP SUGAR

¼ CUP GIN

¼ CUP SWEET VERMOUTH

¼ CUP CAMPARI

2½ CUPS FRESH PINK GRAPEFRUIT JUICE

PINCH OF SALT

Combine the water and sugar in a heavy saucepan and bring to a boil over medium-high heat. Remove from the heat and stir in the remaining ingredients. Let cool to room temperature, then pour into ice-pop molds and freeze according to the manufacturer's instructions.

NEGRONI CHEESECAKE

MONICA BERG, POLLEN STREET SOCIAL, LONDON

Monica created this recipe when she worked at Aqua Vitae in Oslo, Norway. I first met her a few years ago when visiting the good folk at G'Vine Gin in Cognac, France, where we had some damned good chin-wags and capped off the week with a drunken yoga session at around midnight. She now works at the Pollen Street Social in London, where she can keep a close eye on her beau, Alex Kratena of London's Artesian bar. I think of them as the royal family of cocktailians in the UK. Back when Monica was still working in Oslo, she noted that the Negroni Cheesecake basically started out as a joke but became a tradition for birthdays and staff parties. Note that the raspberry-infused Campari for the topping must rest overnight, so plan accordingly.

MAKES 8 TO 12 SERVINGS

TOPPING
3½ OUNCES FRESH RASPBERRIES

⅔ CUP CAMPARI

3 OUNCES RASPBERRY GELATIN MIX

CRUST
8 OUNCES GRAHAM CRACKERS, CRUMBLED

9 TABLESPOONS BUTTER, MELTED

1 TABLESPOON PLUS 1 TEASPOON VERMOUTH REDUCTION (RECIPE FOLLOWS)

FILLING
5 TO 6 SHEETS GELATIN

⅔ CUP FRESH ORANGE JUICE

7 OUNCES CREAM CHEESE, AT ROOM TEMPERATURE

1 CUP SOUR CREAM

5 TABLESPOONS POWDERED SUGAR, OR MORE FOR A SWEETER CHEESECAKE

2 OUNCES GIN, PREFERABLY WITH STRONG JUNIPER NOTES

1 DROP VANILLA EXTRACT

1½ CUPS WHIPPING CREAM

To make the topping, put the raspberries in a container with a lid. Pour in the Campari, cover, and refrigerate overnight.

Make the gelatin according to the package instructions, replacing a little less than half of the ice water with the Campari mixture. Chill until cold but not set.

To make the crust, combine the graham cracker crumbs, butter, and Vermouth Reduction in a bowl and mix well. Press the mixture into the bottom and up the sides of a 9- to 10-inch nonstick springform pan. Refrigerate the crust while you make the filling.

To make the filling, combine the gelatin sheets and orange juice in a large bowl and let sit until the gelatin is completely dissolved. Add the cream cheese and stir to combine. Add the sour cream, powdered sugar, gin, and vanilla extract and stir until thoroughly blended.

In a separate bowl, beat the whipping cream until soft peaks form. Gradually fold the whipped cream into the cream cheese mixture.

To assemble the cheesecake, pour the filling into the chilled crust and refrigerate until set, at least 3 hours. Pour the partially set gelatin mixture over the top and return to the refrigerator overnight.

VERMOUTH REDUCTION

1 SCANT CUP DEMERARA SUGAR

1 (750 ML) BOTTLE SWEET VERMOUTH

Combine the sugar and vermouth in a heavy, nonreactive saucepan over medium-high heat. Cook, stirring constantly, until the sugar is dissolved and the mixture begins to simmer. Lower the heat to medium and cook, stirring frequently, until reduced by about half (to approximately 1½ cups), about 15 to 20 minutes. Let cool before using.

BOY, DOES HE LOVE HIS NEGRONIS!

"For those of you who don't already know, gaz is a lover, not a fighter, and boy, does he love his Negronis! I was a finalist in a competition that gaz was judging earlier this year. While the rest of the panel members were seeking a respite by drinking water between tasting cocktails, lo and behold, our gaz was cleansing his palate (and very thoroughly, I might add) with Negronis. Now, that's what I call dedication!"

—FRANKY MARSHALL, the Monkey Bar, New York City

IT'S A RISKY PROCEDURE

"I love the Negroni for a lot of reasons, one of which is that it's a drink that's possible to order in almost any dive bar, though it's a risky procedure. Even if bartenders don't know what it is, you just tell them equal parts on the rocks, and from there the adventure begins. How old and rancid is that bottle of Stock sweet vermouth? How badly will they pour three 'equal' parts? Forrest Gump's mom was wrong. Life isn't like a box of chocolates; it's like a Negroni in a dive bar. You just never know what you're gonna get!"

—PHIL WARD, Mayahuel, New York City

PARSON'S NEGRONI SLUSHY

CHARLIE SCHOTT, BAR MANAGER AND PRINCIPLE BARTENDER,
PARSON'S CHICKEN AND FISH, CHICAGO

Charlie kindly adjusted Parson's recipe for this slushy, figuring that you probably don't have a slushy machine. The recipe here works well in a blender. Or, if you have an ice cream machine, add around 4½ ounces of water for the best results. The Luxardo Bitter, by the way, brings a nice ripe cherry note to the potion.

MAKES 2 OR 3 SERVINGS

2 OUNCES LETHERBEE GIN

2 OUNCES SWEET VERMOUTH

2 OUNCES LUXARDO BITTER

2½ OUNCES FRESH
GRAPEFRUIT JUICE

2½ OUNCES FRESH ORANGE JUICE

1½ CUPS CRUSHED ICE

GARNISH: FROZEN ORANGE
HALF WHEELS

Put all the ingredients in a blender and process at high speed, stopping occasionally to stir the ingredients together. Continue blending at high speed, adding more crushed ice to achieve the desired consistency. Serve garnished with the frozen orange half wheels.

NEGRONI ICE CREAM

NATASHA CASE AND FREYA ESTRELLER, COOLHAUS, LOS ANGELES

When making this ice cream, use the freshest eggs available for best results. If possible, refrigerate the base for a full 24 hours—the longer, the better. We like to chill our bases in plastic or stainless steel pitchers (with airtight lids) for easy pouring into the ice cream maker after chilling.

MAKES ABOUT 6 SERVINGS

2 CUPS WHOLE MILK	JUICE OF ½ ORANGE
2 CUPS HEAVY CREAM	⅔ OUNCE AVIATION GIN
1¼ CUPS GRANULATED SUGAR	⅔ OUNCE VERMOUTH, PREFERABLY CINZANO OR CARPANO
8 LARGE EGG YOLKS	⅔ OUNCE CAMPARI
ZEST OF 1 ORANGE	PINCH OF SALT

In a large, heavy saucepan, combine the milk, cream, and half of the sugar. Cook over high heat, stirring occasionally, until the mixture comes to a boil, about 5 minutes.

Meanwhile, in a medium bowl, whisk the yolks and the remaining half of the sugar until smooth, heavy, and pale yellow, about 30 seconds.

When the cream mixture just comes to a boil, whisk, then remove from the heat. While whisking constantly, pour half of the cream mixture into the egg yolk mixture in a slow stream and continue whisking until thoroughly blended.

Return the pan to the stove top over low heat. While whisking constantly, slowly pour the cream mixture back into the pan. Switch to a wooden spoon, and cook, stirring constantly, until the mixture registers between 165° and 180° Fahrenheit on an instant-read thermometer, about 2 minutes. Do not heat above 180° Fahrenheit, or the egg yolks will set up. The mixture should be steaming but not boiling, and slightly thickened— enough to coat the back of a spoon. If you blow on the back of the spoon and the mixture ripples, you've got the right consistency.

Pour the mixture into a clean, airtight container. Cover and refrigerate for at least 12 hours and no longer than 5 days before using.

Add the orange zest and juice and stir until combined. Pour into an ice cream maker and process according to the manufacturer's instructions until the ice cream takes on a consistency like soft-serve ice cream. Add the gin, vermouth, Campari, and salt and process for several more minutes, until the consistency is once again like soft-serve ice cream. (The alcohol will initially reverse the freezing process.)

Remove from the ice cream maker and store in a sealed container in the freezer for at least 2 hours before serving.

NEGRONI CARAMEL POPCORN

STEPHEN LEE, PRIVATE DINING DIRECTOR,
PERBACCO RISTORANTE AND BAR, SAN FRANCISCO

Many thanks to Stephen for sending me this recipe for Perbacco's spectacular Negroni popcorn.

MAKES ABOUT 8 SERVINGS

8 CUPS POPPED POPCORN

1 CUP GRANULATED SUGAR

2 TABLESPOONS GIN SALT (RECIPE FOLLOWS)

1 CUP CAMPARI

1/2 CUP SWEET VERMOUTH

1/4 CUP WATER

2 TABLESPOONS UNSALTED BUTTER

2 TABLESPOONS HONEY

4 TEASPOONS CORN SYRUP

1 ORANGE TWIST

1/2 TEASPOON BAKING SODA

Line a sheet pan with parchment paper. Oil the parchment paper and the sides of the baking sheet. Put the popcorn in a large bowl.

Combine the sugar, Gin Salt, Campari, vermouth, water, butter, honey, corn syrup, and orange twist in a heavy saucepan over medium heat. Cook, stirring frequently, until golden brown. Stir in the baking soda.

Drizzle the mixture over the popcorn and toss gently until evenly coated. Transfer to the prepared pan and spread in a thin layer, tossing until cool. Enjoy immediately, or store in an airtight container.

GIN SALT

1 TEASPOON JUNIPER BERRIES

¾ TEASPOON CORIANDER SEEDS

½ TEASPOON CARDAMOM SEEDS

¼ TEASPOON FENNEL SEEDS

1 TEASPOON ANISE SEEDS

SCANT ¼ TEASPOON WHITE
PEPPERCORNS

½ STAR ANISE POD

¼ TEASPOON GROUND DRY GINGER

1½ TEASPOONS DRIED MANDARIN
ORANGE PEEL

2 TABLESPOONS PLUS ½ TEASPOON
FINE SEA SALT

Combine everything except the salt in a blender, spice grinder, or clean coffee mill and process until very fine. Pass through a fine-mesh sieve to remove any larger pieces. Mix with the salt.

CREDITS AND THANKS

Agent Provocateur: Francesco Lafranconi, Southern Wine & Spirits, Las Vegas, NV

Alexandria Hotel Cocktail, aka Spring Street District Cocktail: Marcos Tello, The Varnish, Los Angeles, CA

Barrel-Aged Negronis: Jeffrey Morgenthaler, Clyde Common, Portland, OR

Belfast Bastard, a Lucien Gaudin Variation: Jack McGarry, The Dead Rabbit, New York, NY

Bitter End: Ted Kilgore, Taste Bar and Last Word Cocktail Consulting, St. Louis, MO

Bitter French: Philip Ward, Mayahuel, New York, NY

Bittersweet Symphony: Jeffrey Morgenthaler, bar manager, Clyde Common, Portland, OR

Blackberry Bitter: Dani Tatarin, Keefer Bar, Vancouver, Canada

Bottecchia: Kevin Burke, head barkeep, Colt & Gray, Denver, CO

Boulevardier: Erskine Gwynne

Brazilevardier: Matty Durgin, Green Russel Bar, Denver, CO

Bridgetown Stomp: Julie Reiner, Clover Club, Flatiron Lounge, Lani Kai, New York, NY

Brooklyn Heights: Maxwell Britten, New York, NY

Buñueloni: Jeff "Beachbum" Berry

Camillo in Xela: Max La Rocca, host of the popular mixology blog *Listen to the Ice*

Caricature Cocktail: gaz regan

Corn Goddess: David Wondrich

Dog and Pony: Jill Saunders, Tanqueray Brand Ambassador, UK

D.O.M.E. Negroni: Mihai Fetcu, Bistro de l'Arte, Brasov, Romania

Drunk Uncle: Shawn Soole, Little Jumbo Restaurant & Bar, Victoria, Canada

East India Negroni: Jim Meehan, PDT, New York, NY

French Negroni: Ludovic Miazga, France

Gaijin: Kirsti Kinservik, Alexander Valley Bar, Healdsburg, CA

GFE Negroni: Jim Geurts, Triple J. Bar, Bilzen, Belgium

House of Payne: Phil Ward, Mayahuel, New York, NY

Knickroni: Frederic Yarm, *Cocktail Virgin* blog, Somerville, MA

Lemon Balm Negroni: Shawn Soole, Little Jumbo Restaurant & Bar, Victoria, Canada

Maximo di Negroni: Shawn Soole, Little Jumbo Restaurant & Bar Victoria, Canada

Mela d'Alba: Andrew Friedman, Liberty, Seattle, WA

Minimo di Negroni: Shawn Soole, Little Jumbo Restaurant & Bar, Victoria, Canada

My Fave!: Moses Laboy, Red Rooster, New York, NY

My Old Pal: *Barflies and Cocktails*

Negroni Caramel Popcorn: Stephen Lee, private dining director, Perbacco Ristorante and Bar, San Francisco, CA

Negroni Cheesecake: Monica Berg, Pollen Street Social, London, UK

Negroni Club: Mauro Mahjoub's Negroni Club, Munich, Germany

Negroni de Provence: Nicolas de Soto, head bartender, Experimental Cocktail Club, New York, NY

Negroni del Nonno: Mauro Mahjoub's Negroni Club, Munich, Germany

Negroni Fizz: Grace Roth, Adirondack / Kinfolk 94, Brooklyn, NY

Negroni Futurista: Mauro Mahjoub Negroni Club, Munich, Germany

Negroni Hors Pair: Colin Peter Field, the Hemingway Bar at the Ritz, Paris, France

Negroni Ice Cream: Natasha Case and Freya Estreller, CoolHaus, Los Angeles, CA

Negroni Popsicle: Jake Godby, chef and owner, Humphry Slocombe Ice Cream, San Francisco, CA

Oaxaca Negroni: Josh Trabulsi, Burritt Room, San Francisco, CA

Parson's Negroni Slushy: Charlie Schott, bar manager and principle bartender, Parson's Chicken and Fish, Chicago, IL

Pepper Negroni: Mixologist Jason Walsh, bar consultant, New York, NY

Piscoroni: gaz regan

Pizza Negroni: Morgan Schick, Trick Dog, San Francisco, SF

Pousse-Port Negroni: Domingo-Martin Barreres, mixologist, Market by Jean Georges, W Hotel, Boston, MA

Southpaw: Joseph Boley, Red House, Paris, France

Stiletta: Phil Ward, Mayahuel, New York, NY

Strawberry Negroni: Jared Brown and Anistatia Miller, Mixellany, Ltd., London, UK

Street & Smith: Katie Stipe, New York, NY

Unusual Negroni: Charlotte Voisey, mixologist with William Grant & Sons, US

White Negroni: Eric Alperin, co-owner of the Varnish, Los Angeles, CA

White Negroni with Campari Caviar: Brian Felley and Mo Hodges, Benjamin~Cooper, San Francisco, CA

━━━

I'd be remiss if I didn't give a special shout-out the following folk, who opened their doors and mixed drinks so that photographer Kelly Puleio could work her magic with the photographs. Thanks, everyone. It's my round when I see you.

Brian Felley and Mo Hodges of the forthcoming Benjamin~Cooper

Erika Frey of Campo Fina, Healdsburg, CA

Ethan Terry of the Alembic, San Francisco, CA

Jessica Maria, owner of the Hotsy Totsy, Albany, CA

Josh Trabulsi of Burritt Room + Tavern, San Francisco, CA

Kim Rosselle of Trick Dog, San Francisco, CA

Kirsti Kinservik of Alexander Valley Bar, Healdsburg, CA

INDEX

Published in the United States by Ten Speed Press, an imprint of the
Crown Publishing Group, a division of Random House LLC, a Penguin
Random House Company, New York.
www.crownpublishing.com
www.tenspeed.com

Ten Speed Press and the Ten Speed Press colophon are registered
trademarks of Random House LLC.

Originally published in Great Britain in different form by Mixellany
Limited, Cheltenham, in 2013.

Grateful acknowledgment is made to Natasha Case, Freya Estreller,
Kathleen Squires, and Houghton Mifflin Harcourt for the recipe
"Negroni Ice Cream" from *The Coolhaus Ice Cream Book*, copyright
© 2014 by Natasha Case and Freya Estreller with Kathleen Squires.
Adapted by permission of Houghton Mifflin Harcourt

Library of Congress Cataloging-in-Publication Data

Regan, Gary.
The negroni : drinking to la dolce vita, with recipes and lore / Gary "Gaz"
Regan ; photography by Kelly Puleio. —First American edition.
    pages cm
Includes index.
1. Cocktails. 2. Negroni, Camillo, 1868-1934. I. Title.
TX951.R3645 2015
641.87'4—dc23

                    2014034991

Hardcover ISBN: 978-1-60774-779-6

eBook ISBN: 978-1-60774-780-2

Printed in China

Design by Margaux Keres

Hand drawn type by Christina Jirachachavalwong

10 9 8 7 6 5 4 3 2 1

First Edition